SpringerBriefs in Political Science

AF180800

More information about this series at http://www.springer.com/series/8871

James P. Howard, II

Socioeconomic Effects of the National Flood Insurance Program

Springer

James P. Howard, II
Columbia, MD, USA

ISSN 2191-5466 ISSN 2191-5474 (electronic)
SpringerBriefs in Political Science
ISBN 978-3-319-29062-1 ISBN 978-3-319-29063-8 (eBook)
DOI 10.1007/978-3-319-29063-8

Library of Congress Control Number: 2016937005

Printed on acid-free paper

This Springer imprint is published by Springer Nature
The registered company is Springer International Publishing AG Switzerland

For Nina, Chase, and Beatrix

Foreword

Let a policy-oriented data scientist approach a problem of long standing and something new can happen. *Socioeconomic Effects of the National Flood Insurance Program* is the first synthesis of this government-run behemoth that insures from flood damages over 5 million people and 1 trillion dollars in property value. There is something in here for almost everyone interested in policy about flooding.

- Government budget watchers can find how the program likely shifted half a billion dollars a year from the federal budget back onto beneficiaries, but at the same time, government policies keep the program from being self-sufficient when particularly large disasters strike such as Hurricanes Katrina and Sandy.
- Consumer watch dogs and insurance and policy analysts can find new estimates of what homeowners in flood-prone areas think the program is actually worth.
- Students of behavior can find the oddities of how people respond to a perennial risk and the geographic distribution of who pays in and who gets paid.
- Those seeking efficiency in government can find quantitative estimates in a framework endorsed by presidential executive orders, a benefit-cost analysis.

But the total is greater than the sum of its parts. James has created a transparent, analytical Christmas tree on which readers of all persuasions can hang their own perspective and data. James's analysis may not be the last word, but what would be on such a large topic affecting so many? Like the best of analyses, he has provided a structure and estimates that frame the conceptual and quantitative debate.

When I mentioned James's topic to the head of an institute specializing in hazards such a flooding, I was emphatically told the topic was much too broad. But James pulled it off with distinction in a model "as simple as possible but no simpler." I highly recommend a careful read.

Founding editor, *Journal of Benefit-Cost Analysis* Scott Farrow, Ph.D.
Former Chief Economist
U.S. Government Accountability Office

Preface

This evaluation came from my doctoral research at the University of Maryland, Baltimore County. I had approached Scott Farrow, who would later become my advisor about writing my dissertation on benefit-cost analysis (BCA). He responded with a few possibilities, but one about the National Flood Insurance Program (NFIP) jumped out at me. I had never experienced a flood event nor did I live particularly close to water, but the project seemed important and challenging.

The NFIP has been the subject of a great deal of research following Hurricane Katrina. Katrina exposed the large risks associated with coastal living, and many of the payments necessary to support Katrina's victims came from the NFIP. Much of the research has focused on the risk to the government and the risk to the environment. All of these analyses inform this evaluation. With this evaluation, the research is synthesized and reduced to estimates of the net social benefits (NSB) of the NFIP.

Using BCA provides a unique lens to evaluate any program. BCA provides the first estimate of the long-term benefits to society, but can do much more. BCA, coupled with distributionally weighting, provides a distributional analysis of the NFIP. With that evaluation, we can confirm the results of other analyses and show that the NFIP's benefits flow more toward higher-income regions. We can also adapt the BCA method to show the effects of the program on the government's finances, an open question.

The framework developed here can be adapted to other governmental programs, especially insurance programs. The framework can also be extended to revise the analysis of the NFIP. Both are options for future exploration and I encourage researchers to explore them.

While the NFIP has been and will be the target of reform efforts, this evaluation is not designed to support or detract from any particular effort. The policy is evaluated as-is, and recommendations on how to adapt the analysis for reform efforts are provided. However, no policy pronouncements about "what should be done" are made here. The result, I hope, is a clean and honest evaluation of the NFIP that can provide framework and guidance to future scholars and policymakers.

I would first like to thank my doctoral adviser, Scott Farrow, for his guidance in my dissertation and this book. Both owe their existence to his support. I would also like to thank the members of my committee, Marv Mandell, Andy Miller, Porter Hoagland, and Craig Landry. I would like to thank the University of Maryland Baltimore County Graduate Student Association for providing grant funding to support this research.

The Federal Emergency Management Agency (FEMA) provided extensive data to make this dissertation possible. At FEMA, both Timothy Scoville and Zachary Usher provided access to the FEMA financial and grant data, respectively. In addition, Craig Landry provided data used to estimate the consumer surplus of the NFIP.

I would like to thank my editor, Lorraine Klimowich, who saw this project through at Springer. I would also like to thank Kevin Halligan who managed production at Springer.

Finally, I would like to thank my family. Nina was there at every step and Chase and Beatrix lived their entire lives with "Daddy's big book." They asked, when it was over, if it meant the beach repairs they had watched in Delaware were over now that the book was.

Columbia, MD, USA James P. Howard, II
December 1, 2015

Contents

Acronyms

AIR	American Institutes for Research
BCA	benefit-cost analysis
BCR	benefit-cost ratio
BLS	Bureau of Labor Statistics
BOB	United States Bureau of the Budget
BOR	Bureau of Reclamation
BWFIRA	Biggert-Waters Flood Insurance Reform Act of 2012
CBRA	Coastal Barrier Resources Act of 1982
CFHA	Coastal Flood Hazard Area
CMR	constant maturity rate
CPI	Consumer Price Index
CRS	Community Rating System
CVM	contingent valuation method
DOJ	United States Department of Justice
DRA	Disaster Relief Act of 1974
EO 12127	Executive Order 12127
EO 12866	Executive Order 12866
EO 13563	Executive Order 13563
FCA	Flood Control Act of 1936
FDPA	Flood Disaster Protection Act of 1973
FEMA	Federal Emergency Management Agency

FFIA	Federal Flood Insurance Act of 1956
FIRA	Flood Insurance Reform Act of 2004
FIRM	Flood Insurance Rate Map
FIRMA	Flood Insurance Reform and Modernization Act of 2008
FIRPA	Flood Insurance Reform Priorities Act of 2010
FMA	Flood Mitigation Assistance
GIS	geographic information systems
ICC	Increased Cost Compliance
MCS	Monte Carlo simulation
METB	marginal excess tax burden
MLE	maximum-likelihood estimation
MLS	Multiple Listing Service
MMC	Multihazard Mitigation Council
NAS	National Academy of Science
NFIA	National Flood Insurance Act of 1968
NFIF	National Flood Insurance Fund
NFIP	National Flood Insurance Program
NFIRA	National Flood Insurance Reform Act of 1994
NIBS	National Institute of Building Sciences
NRC	National Research Council
NRCS	Natural Resources Conservation Service
NSB	net social benefits
OLS	ordinary least squares
OMB	Office of Management and Budget
RPM	revealed preferences method
SDR	social discount rate
SFHA	Special Flood Hazard Area
TVA	Tennessee Valley Authority
USACE	United States Army Corps of Engineers
USCB	United States Census Bureau

WRC	United States Water Resources Council
WTP	willingness-to-pay
WYO	Write Your Own

Chapter 1
Introduction

The National Flood Insurance Program (NFIP) rises to the top of the political agenda following major hurricanes and flood events. The program has been through several reform cycles over more than four decades and has been changed or expanded each time. Whether or not this program has provided net benefits to the country or the government is not well understood. This analysis provides the first comprehensive benefit-cost analysis (BCA) at the NFIP and its related programs.

The NFIP is a federal program that provides flood insurance to homeowners and businesses. Congress created the NFIP in 1968 because the private insurance market did not provide any policies against flood events and the federal government found itself in the frequent position of appropriating emergency funds to assist in flood recovery and rebuilding. Today, the Federal Emergency Management Agency (FEMA) manages the NFIP and the Flood Mitigation Assistance (FMA) program. The FMA program was created in the mid-1990s in response to large hurricane-related losses and provides grants to state and local governments for projects to reduce the damage caused by floods through mitigation and prevention projects. Together, these two public programs form the core of the US flood mitigation and recovery policy.

1.1 Background and Significance

The NFIP has grown into the largest single-hazard insurer in the USA. The program provides more than a trillion dollars of insurance coverage to more than 5 million policyholders. Despite the size of the NFIP, the risks of the program are concentrated. For example, more than 40 % of the program's policies insure properties in Florida. Florida's higher risk, vis-à-vis other states, for hurricane-related flooding exposes the NFIP to concentrated geographic risks.

J. Howard, II, *Socioeconomic Effects of the National Flood Insurance Program*, SpringerBriefs in Political Science, DOI 10.1007/978-3-319-29063-8_1

The NFIP is unable to manage that geographic risk effectively due to two policies. The first policy provides discounted flood insurance to individuals who meet certain conditions and to those whose homes were built before a 1973 legal change. The second policy is that FEMA, who also manages the Flood Insurance Rate Map (FIRM), which decides flood insurance pricing, has not updated the FIRM for many years and may have used incorrect flood data in some places. Both policies decrease insurance premium rates below the actuarially fair rate, the rate equivalent to the expected losses for the property. As a result, the NFIP does not receive enough revenue to pay for insurance claims.

While the NFIP is often subject to formal study, an evaluation showing the net social benefits (NSB) of the NFIP has not been conducted. Neither is the full effect of the program on the federal budget understood. At the individual policyholder level, the value of an NFIP policy is not known and neither is how the costs and benefits are distributed across economic classes. This analysis will answer each of these questions and is significant due to the political, economic, and social context of the program in the USA.

The main constituency groups of the NFIP are the taxpayers of the USA and the NFIP's policyholders. It is not clear if the government would ensure the financial stability of the NFIP if the program were insolvent. Accordingly, understanding the benefits and costs of the NFIP is useful to understand the effect on government finances. In addition, Congress has considered many potential changes to the program such as adding wind insurance, privatizing the program, or other structural changes. Finally, understanding the distributional effects of the program would be useful to the policy-making process by showing how the policy affects those with lower income.

1.2 Topic and Method

This analysis will evaluate the social benefits of the NFIP and FMA programs using BCA. This analysis will develop the methodology of BCA as applied to the NFIP and FMA programs and generate estimates of the NSB for those programs. The analysis will be in four stages. The first stage is an estimate of the consumer surplus for flood insurance, which is necessary to measure the benefit consumers receive from the program. The second stage is a retrospective BCA of the NFIP covering the period from 1996 through 2010. The third stage is a distributionally weighted BCA, in which effects are weighted according to the income of the recipient's home county. The fourth stage will estimate the effect of the NFIP on the federal budget. Although this study is retrospective, the results can inform policy decisions about flood risk and other government-run insurance programs, from an *ex ante* perspective. For instance, these results can provide a baseline against which to measure potential changes to the NFIP.

The analysis is constrained by the data available. The first of these constraints drives the analytical viewpoint to a retrospective analysis. There are historical data for the NFIP program starting in 1977, when FEMA began administering the program. There is information on the FMA grants program starting in 1996, when FEMA began the grant-making process to local jurisdictions for flood mitigation. These data lend themselves to retrospective analysis given the data availability and the unpredictable nature of both flood events and Congressional funding for individual programs. Therefore, this analysis will only look at the time period from 1996 through 2010, reflecting the period for which data are best available.

Closely related to the first constraint, the second constraint focuses on data granularity. The data for premiums and claims for the NFIP is given at the county level. Across the USA, counties vary in size and population density and are not necessarily uniformly comparable. Nevertheless, FEMA's NFIP financial information is at the county level. FMA program grants are generally at the county level, as well. Accordingly, a county-level analysis is the most provident vehicle for understanding the NFIP using these data.

1.3 Analytical Viewpoint and Assumptions

This analysis begins with a set of assumptions that frame the analysis and subsequent discussion and stem both from the data available and from the behavior of actors within the economic, social, and political constraints of the NFIP and FMA programs. The major underlying assumptions are described below, and their effect is explained in the analysis, discussion, and conclusions.

A major assumption is governmental behavior in the absence of the NFIP. As described in Chap. 2, the US government routinely offered private disaster relief bills for major disasters before the introduction of the NFIP. This was true for flood disasters and continued after the introduction of the NFIP when the flood insurance program was insufficient to provide full recovery to affected property owners. This leads to the assumption that if the NFIP did not exist, then the federal government would, through private relief bills, continue to provide aid for disaster victims. A related assumption is that the government would pay for this ad hocdisaster relief through general taxes. Further, this assumption is refined to state that the government's ad hocdisaster relief would be equivalent to the amount paid by flood insurance claims. This is based on the motivation behind the NFIP to share the cost of flood recovery with beneficiaries of that recovery funding.

This assumption about the government's behavior in the absence of the NFIP has two important implications. The first implication is that the government would have to raise the funds to pay for the ad hocflood relief via taxes. These taxes have an associated marginal excess tax burden (METB) and that is a cost to the overall economy. The second implication is that the environmental effects, both with and without the NFIP, are identical. Both of these implications are explored in the analysis.

A second assumption is that insurance companies participating in the NFIP's Write Your Own (WYO) program do not benefit from doing so. This assumption underlies the value of the administrative fees paid to insurance companies and whether insurance companies profit from the administration of the NFIP. When assuming insurance companies do not profit from the WYO program, the benefits are reduced for producers in the analysis.

These two assumptions are the key to simplifying the analysis and making it possible to analyze the program in a clear and coherent manner. However, both assumptions are subject to review and are tested through sensitivity analysis to determine the effect of each on the results.

A final assumption is that NFIP borrowing is costless. In general, the NFIP can borrow from the US Treasury to fund any shortfalls necessary to pay claims. However, this analysis will not disaggregate NFIP-related federal borrowing from general federal borrowing whose effect on the broader economy is controversial and unresolved (Hubbard 2012).

These assumptions frame the analysis and structure the interpretation of results. These assumptions also guide the estimation of the consumer surplus for flood insurance found in Chap. 4. The net effect of these assumptions is to focus analysis on the interaction between the consumer surplus for flood insurance and the change in government revenue from the program.

1.4 Expected Outcomes

This research on the NFIP will result in a deeper understanding of NFIP and provide a framework for modeling governmental insurance programs. If the results suggest that the NFIP has provided benefits exceeding its costs over the study period, then the program is likely to continue doing so, provided no substantial changes are made to the program's implementation and the time period analyzed is representative of the long-term flood risk. It would also suggest that programs to provide or subsidize insurance against other types of natural disasters could replicate the model provided by the NFIP. It may also provide a model in creating flood or disaster insurance programs in other nations with underdeveloped private insurance markets or chronic recurrence of certain types of disasters. Finally, the results can provide information to policymakers working on NFIP-related issues, such as the insurance subsidy for policyholders.

If the results suggest that the NFIP has not provided sufficient benefits to exceed the costs to society, then the program is opened to questions about its efficiency and efficacy. This may also result in challenges to redesign, scale down, or scale back the NFIP. In addition to challenging the NFIP and expansions to the NFIP, similar programs should also come under greater scrutiny before being adopted and implemented. Finally, if the NFIP does not pass a benefit–cost test, then the role of the private market and its ability to deliver insurance services demanded by customers should also be reviewed to determine the most effective means of providing insurance.

Lastly, this study can set the path for future research on the NFIP. Numerous evidence-based assumptions will be used which may be improved upon. This effort can be the framework for more detailed analyses of the distributional effects of the NFIP or more detailed analyses of the financial and economic implications of the program. If the program should change, this analytical framework may be reapplied to understand both the social costs and the distributional effects of the revised program.

1.5 Organization of This Book

This book is divided into chapters organized around the distinct research questions considered. Chapter 2 provides an outline of the prior research and literature on the NFIP and the FMA programs.

Chapter 3 establishes a research design for estimating the NSB of the NFIP and FMA programs. In addition, this chapter provides a sufficient statistic for estimating the NSB based on available financial and economic data for the programs. Chapter 4 estimates the consumer surplus for flood insurance through the NFIP. Chapter 5 estimates the NSB as described in Chap. 3, provides a sensitivity analysis, and discusses the results.

Chapter 6 provides a revised research design, based on the previous design, describing a distributionally weighted BCA that is weighted by local jurisdiction income. The chapter also implements that research design and provides a sensitivity analysis and results discussion.

Chapter 7 describes a restricted research design that analyzes the change in the federal government's revenue from the effect of the NFIP and FMA programs on government finances. The chapter also implements that research design and provides a sensitivity analysis and results discussion.

Chapter 8 provides conclusions and places the results of these analyses into context, including limitations and directions for future research. Several appendices describing the datasets used, providing example data, and a brief timeline of the NFIP and FMA programs are included following these analyses.

Chapter 2
Literature Review

2.1 The National Flood Insurance Program

In 1966, Gilbert White led a task force for the United States Bureau of the Budget (BOB), forerunner of the modern Office of Management and Budget (OMB), that recommended a comprehensive national approach to mitigating private flood losses through an insurance program (Rumsey 2010, 56–63). White had suggested the idea as early as his 1942 dissertation on floodplain management (White 1942, 202–204). The task force's report recommended many of the features associated with the National Flood Insurance Program (NFIP) today, such as mapping of the floodplain and the management of floodplain development. However, the task force's report also included a note suggesting national flood insurance may lead to aggravated flood losses by encouraging unsound building in flood-prone areas. The task force's recommendations were implemented in 1968 and, since then, the NFIP has grown into a large monoline insurer with more than 1 trillion dollars in insured assets (Congressional Budget Office 2009, 1). Since 1977, Federal Emergency Management Agency (FEMA) has administered the program.

2.1.1 Background of the National Flood Insurance Program

The 100-year flood is a flood event with a 1 % annual exceedance probability each year (United States Geological Survey 2010). Smaller floods are more likely and larger floods are also possible, though less likely. The 100-year flood is a measure of the intensity of flooding, not the frequency. The associated 100-year floodplain is the resulting area inundated by a 100-year flood, typically along the coast or riverbanks. The 100-year recurrence interval rate is now a bright line in flood planning. In this study, references to the floodplain refer to the 100-year floodplain unless otherwise specified.

J. Howard, II, *Socioeconomic Effects of the National Flood Insurance Program*, SpringerBriefs in Political Science, DOI 10.1007/978-3-319-29063-8_2

FEMA assesses risk and determines premiums for the NFIP through the Flood Insurance Rate Map (FIRM) using historical flood data. The risk assessment process is similar to techniques used by the private insurance market. Contiguous areas with similar risk profiles are then aggregated into areas called flood zones; participants in the NFIP are assessed a premium based on their flood zone and associated risk profile (Burby 2001). FEMA designates the area on the floodplain as the Special Flood Hazard Area (SFHA). If they have a federally financed mortgage, policyholders for property within the SFHA pay a higher premium for NFIP insurance and are required to purchase flood insurance through the NFIP (Michel-Kerjan et al. 2012). Federally financed loans include loans issued by federally regulated banks, loans issued directly by a federal agency, or conforming loans for repurchase by a federal housing finance agency.

The NFIP premiums are held in a dedicated fund, called the National Flood Insurance Fund (NFIF), managed by the US Treasury for the benefit of the NFIP (Brown 2010b, 5). FEMA can invest the assets of the NFIF only in obligations of the US government or investments which are guaranteed by the USA. Congress considers the NFIP an enterprise activity of the federal government. As a result, the debts of the NFIP do not directly add to the national debt, though Treasury borrowing to support the NFIP may indirectly increase the debt. Further, Congress does not limit NFIP claims through the normal budgetary process.

The NFIP is primarily self-financed through premiums. If the premiums paid to the NFIP held in the NFIF are insufficient to cover current claims against the NFIP, the Director of the NFIP may borrow from the US Treasury sufficient funds to pay expenses. The NFIP does not purchase reinsurance through the private market to reduce its dependency on Treasury loans, though Congress has not prohibited such purchases. When necessary, the NFIP has used its line of credit to pay flood insurance claims (Brown 2010b, 5).

The NFIP is not actuarially sound due to two constraints imposed by Congress (Congressional Budget Office 2009, 3). First, older dwellings receive a subsidized premium rate and are not required to meet improved building and planning standards. Second, the risk for extremely rare and severe events may not be adequately accounted for in the premium (Bingham et al. 2006, 61). The constraints lead the NFIP to collect insufficient revenue through premiums and investment of retained earnings to meet expected expenses. The NFIP's expenses are primarily payments of insurance claims to policyholders and administrative overhead fees paid to insurance brokers, who provide local administrative services on behalf of FEMA through the Write Your Own (WYO) program. NFIP rates are actuarially determined based on the presumption that all insured properties meet the SFHA building standards. If a property does not meet the SFHA building standards, it has less resiliency against a flood and is therefore at greater risk.

Congress created the Flood Mitigation Assistance (FMA) program to reduce the disaster assistance costs to the federal government caused by flooding. FEMA implements a program for flood damage mitigation as part of the NFIP. FEMA partners with states and local communities through the FMA program to develop methods for reducing the risk of flood damage (Bullock et al. 2006, 277). Another goal of the FMA program was to reduce the cost of claims for flood-related losses. The FMA program operates through grants for flood mitigation planning and implementation. The NFIP funds FMA grants through the NFIF.

Participants need to be eligible to join the NFIP and may only join if their property is in a community meeting certain requirements for flood mitigation and building codes, both of which increase the resiliency of the community to floods by decreasing their frequency and effect. NFIP participants were limited to 250,000 dollars of flood insurance coverage per claim during the study period. The coverage limit is not inflation-indexed. FEMA sets the coverage limit and periodically adjusts it to account for increased housing values.

NFIP policyholders in Florida make up more than 40 % of all policyholders and are frequently studied as part of NFIP analyses. Michel-Kerjan and Kousky (2010) used anonymized policyholder data provided by FEMA to answer questions about the flood insurance market. Michel-Kerjan and Kousky found 80 % of all NFIP policies were for single family homes. Further, while the NFIP has deep penetration within the 100-year floodplain, due to the mandatory purchase requirements; more than 18 % of the policies in force in Florida were outside the 500-year floodplain, where there is presumptively less risk of flooding. In addition, Michel-Kerjan and Kousky found 73 % of homeowners had policies reflecting less than the maximum coverage. Finally, Michel-Kerjan and Kousky note the number of policyholders increased following 2004, a year with an exceptionally high number of hurricanes striking the state, consistent with other studies linking purchases to flood experience.

There is also an element of community participation in the NFIP. Property owners in communities which do not participate are ineligible to purchase NFIP policies, which has a carry-over effect of denying access to federally subsidized mortgages and other property-related programs (Shilling et al. 1989). Participating communities agree to adopt building and land use codes recommended by FEMA to reduce the flood hazard risk within the community (Burby 2001; Burby and French 1981). When communities meet the minimum standards, property owners can join the NFIP. While building and planning codes may reduce potential damages to new construction, zoning and building codes cannot be enforced retroactively against already developed properties. Property owners of property developed before a community joined the NFIP still qualify for a subsidized premium for flood insurance creating a disparity among property owners depending on when their property was developed.

Beyond minimum compliance, FEMA assesses communities through the Community Rating System (CRS) (Brody et al. 2007). Through the CRS, FEMA gives points to local communities for exceeding the minimum standards required to join the NFIP. As a community's points increase, property owners receive a greater discount on flood insurance up to 45 %. However, participating communities tend not to join the CRS program (Landry and Li 2011) and there is little evidence that exceeding FEMA's standards increases resilience or reduces flood damages. Communities can incur expenses in revising and adopting compliant building and land use codes, beyond the cost of meeting revised standards, but communities can receive assistance in complying with community participation requirements by applying for FMA grants from FEMA.

2.1.2 The National Flood Insurance Program and Risk

One of the goals of the NFIP was to reduce the cost to the federal budget for flood recovery and to share recovery costs with the policyholders. In 1794, Congress passed a bill providing compensation to unidentified victims of disasters (Landis 1998). Direct federal disaster relief became common between 1803 and 1947; Moss (1999) notes Congress passed "at least 128 specific legislative acts offering *ad hoc*relief" from flood, fire, and other major disasters. The NFIP policyholders are likely to be the beneficiaries of disaster relief if the NFIP did not exist and a flood occurred.

During the early part of the 1900s, fire insurance providers provided private flood insurance policies, which were similar to general accident policies. However, private insurers abandoned the flood insurance market after a series of floods along the Mississippi River in the late 1920s lead to the collapse of several regional insurance companies (Kunreuther 2006).

Scales (2006) argues the lack of private insurance is a market failure due to several aspects of the flood insurance market. The first aspect is the perceived failure of insurers ability to accurately measure risk of flood. However, the ability to accurately measure flood risk has improved due to the NFIP and its floodplain mapping program. The second aspect is adverse selection inherent in any insurance program. Adverse selection, in the case of the NFIP, describes the phenomenon where property owners with little to no flood risk are less likely to purchase flood insurance than property owners with substantially higher risk. As a result, the average risk of the purchaser pool is higher than it might be if more participants were involved. Additionally, there may be an assumption by some property owners that the government will provide sufficient disaster relief in the form of direct payments to victims of a significant flood event. Scales, based on the work of Kunreuther (2006), claims direct government disaster relief is not a motivating factor for potential policyholders who choose not to purchase flood insurance, suggesting there is no market failure basis for the NFIP.

In 2005, Hurricane Katrina demonstrated federal flood insurance coverage alone was insufficient to secure policyholders following a major flood. Damage from Katrina was caused by both wind and flood, including flood stemming from levee failure. Land protected by a levee is administratively considered outside the floodplain and so has an associated lower-risk profile. Limitations on federal claims and the unwillingness of private insurers to pay for storm-related damage left some policyholders unable or unwilling to rebuild. After the hurricane, affected property owners filed numerous claims against private insurance policies and the NFIP. Private insurers resisted claims by property owners arguing all of the damage to homes in Louisiana and Mississippi was caused by flooding (Horne 2006, 249–253). The existing 250,000 dollar limit on payouts through the NFIP left many without sufficient coverage to be made whole. Accordingly, property owners were unable to completely cover their Katrina-related losses through insurance. Horne cites the case of then Senator Trent Lott of Mississippi who formulated a legal strategy that wind damage was necessary to cause the amount of damage done to his home (Horne 2006, 252), though Lott's efforts were largely unsuccessful (Luebken 2008).

Private insurance and additional federal assistance have been used to rebuild New Orleans after Katrina. Despite the limitations on federal flood insurance claims, Hurricane Katrina still led to almost 17 billion dollars in payments to NFIP policyholders (Cooper and Block 2006, 289), approximately one-third of federal spending on Katrina recovery. Further, private insurance policies paid approximately 30 billion dollars to policyholders in the wake of Katrina for non-flood damage, such as wind damage. According to Comfort et al., total private and public recovery efforts, combined with private donations, were more than 150 billion dollars. The NFIP was approximately one-tenth of all spending for recovery (Comfort et al. 2010).

2.1.3 The Flood Mitigation Program

Congress created the FMA grant program as part of the National Flood Insurance Reform Act of 1994 (NFIRA) with the goal of reducing flood insurance claims under the NFIP (Moss et al. 2009). The NFIRA followed several large storms in the Gulf Coast region in the early 1990s. The FMA program provides grants to state and local jurisdictions for managing flood risks.

The FMA program operates through three overall grant types: project, planning, and technical assistance (Fraser et al. 2006). Project grants fund direct flood mitigation projects, such as dams or beach replenishment. Planning grants fund procedural changes, such as improved building codes, which increase the resiliency of structures to flooding. Technical assistance grants provide administrative funding to state and local jurisdictions for managing the FMA program. Technical assistance grants are similar to project grants and grant recipients can convert them to project grants under certain circumstances. Taken together, the FMA's three grant types reduce the overall risk to the NFIP by ensuring insured properties have some measure of flood protection. The FMA program is not funded from general tax revenues, but instead is funded by a transfer from the NFIF (King 2005, 25). Therefore, NFIP program participants indirectly fund the FMA program, linking the two programs.

Despite the benefits of flood mitigation, it can change the behavior of property owners. Kousky found owners with increased risk are not necessarily more likely to purchase flood insurance, except owners who are directly adjacent to a body of water (Kousky 2008, 105). Significantly, Kousky also found homeowners whose homes are protected by a levee are less likely to purchase flood insurance, despite the failures of the levees to protect New Orleans following Hurricane Katrina or to protect St. Louis during the 1993 Midwest Floods (Kousky 2008, 124–125). FEMA maps will indicate a reduced flood risk for an area protected by a levee if the levee meets NFIP standards for protection. Kousky's findings suggest a certain degree of complacency among prospective policyholders when a flood threat is not readily apparent or believed mitigated. However, the findings regarding levees are open to challenge. Kriesel and Landry (2004) found for coastal residents, a levee, seawall, or other flood protection structure encourages potential NFIP participants to purchase a policy. Like Kousky (2008), Kriesel and Landry conclude homeowners are more likely to purchase insurance as property moves closer to a potential flood source. Kriesel and Landry's results apply to residents in coastal areas whereas Kousky's results were derived from flood risk in St. Louis, Missouri, a riverine flood risk. Homeowners may be more willing to interpret the flood control structure for a coastal flood risk as a warning than they are for a riverine flood risk.

Others may not know of floodplain management concerns. Using a survey conducted among residents in communities participating in the NFIP, 12 % or fewer of responding individuals were aware of building codes to mitigate flood damage or land use regulations to mitigate flood damage. Only 1 % were aware of insurance mechanisms to manage flood risk. Of respondents who purchased flood insurance policies through the NFIP, only a quarter were aware of the subsidies provided by the government (Kunreuther et al. 1978, 213–214, 236). The survey also shows homeowners are not apparently well-informed or directly affected by the effects of neither the NFIP nor floodplain management techniques.

2.1.4 *Floodplain Management, the Environment, and Moral Hazard*

The floodplain provides protection against flood risk. Bullock and Acreman (1999) performed a systematic analysis on the role of wetlands in providing protection, finding a strong link with 23 of 28 studies showing floods delayed or reduced. Similarly, Brody et al. (2007) collected information on the role of wetlands to argue wetlands "provide natural flood mitigation by maintaining a properly functioning water cycle." Increased building on the floodplains and wetlands reduces the protection capacity by decreasing the unbuilt environment.

Some contend the existence of flood insurance encourages building in flood-prone and environmentally sensitive areas as owners insure against losses they would not accept on their own. If the NFIP is shown to encourage building on the wetlands and the floodplain, then this reduces the wetlands and floodplains capacity to protect against flooding. Such building is implicitly subsidized by the NFIP (Cutter and Emrich 2006; McLeman and Smit 2006). Accordingly, if the NFIP did not exist, such building may be reduced due to the lack of subsidized risk taking. Therefore, there is a reasonable claim that the NFIP causes ecological losses.

The willingness or lack of willingness of community managers and property owners to use floodplain maps in making land use decisions also hampers the NFIP's mitigation goals. Since Hurricane Katrina in 2005, researchers have conducted a series of studies to address the question of how the NFIP has influenced development potentially leading to moral hazard. Martin (2008) found evidence that development was directly encouraged by the flood insurance subsidy based on a study of Ocean City, Maryland. NFIP policies for buildings built after 1974 are required to be actuarially sound, but not for structures built before. Prior to the NFIP, the risks associated with replacement cost for structures in Ocean City made them prohibitively expensive to construct (Martin 2008, 54). The presence of insurance allowed Ocean City and other cities on Maryland's Eastern Shore to become vacation destinations for residents in the Baltimore-Washington region through the construction of insurable and insured housing units. Martin (2008) goes on to explain the Coastal Barrier Resources Act of 1982 (CBRA) reduces the NFIP subsidy in high-risk areas through new rules.

Purchasing insurance can also lead to moral hazard, a condition "which occurs when insurance creates incentives for people to behave in inefficient or even fraudulent ways" (Frank 2006, 211). Boulware (2009) argues the NFIP creates a moral hazard by encouraging development through underpriced insurance and underwriting. Through survey results, Boulware (2009) finds survey respondents who perceive a greater flood risk than exists are more likely to voluntarily purchase flood insurance through the NFIP, which the author calls the "operational definition of adverse selection" (Boulware 2009, 163).

The economic effects of the NFIP also appear to include effects in the prices of existing homes. In 1994, Griffith studied the effects of mandatory flood insurance purchase requirements on the real estate market in Abilene, Texas, using policy-in-force data from FEMA and property information from the tax appraisal process. Her study assumed floodplain mapping and purchase requirements together reduce real estate development on the floodplain. However, she discovered while home purchasers do not discount their purchases in the floodplain in response to risk, sellers do discount their price in response to required insurance purchases (Griffith 1994b, 124). She also found mortgage lender-enforcement of flood insurance reduced the purchase price by an average of 4000 dollars.

The Griffith study agrees with a later study by Bin et al. (2008), which showed a significant decrease in the price of sold property located on the designated floodplain. Their results showed a 7.3 % discount in housing values for a property on the 100-year floodplain compared to properties located on the 500-year floodplain, a lower-risk designation (Bin et al. 2008). At the same time, there is also a strong correlation between coastal amenities (beachfront property, views, and cultural activities) and flood risk. An earlier study by Bin and Polasky (2004) also found the effects of Hurricane Floyd, in 1999, increased the discount for properties located on the floodplain.

In other cases, the floodplain may not be considered by planners. For example, in 2001, Pierce County, Washington, including a substantial portion of the Seattle suburbs, undertook comprehensive planning. Though flooding is a primary hazard, land use planning efforts did not consider flooding in the comprehensive plan. One planning professional admitted not knowing "Pierce County was participating in the National Flood Insurance Programme's Community Rating System (CRS) programme" (Godschalk et al. 2003). Though the unnamed planner was also responsible for implementing the comprehensive plan for development, the planner did not take into account floodplain management. A community task force instead developed the comprehensive plan, ignoring floodplain management.

Kousky (2008) found real estate development in Chesterfield County, Missouri, may have been driven by poor information about the flood risk, similar to the situation in Pierce County. Following initial development, new patterns may take hold and be driven by a changed threat perception following a catastrophic flood (Kousky 2008, 182). Kousky notes FEMA has made great strides to make more information about flood risk to specific parcels of land available; however, there is no research available to determine its effectiveness in modifying homeowner behavior.

In addition, courts have limited the ability to enforce federal requirements to manage the floodplain responsibly. In 1985, the United States Department of Justice (DOJ) sued the Parish of St. Bernard, later devastated by Hurricane Katrina, to enforce the flood mitigation requirements of the NFIP. In the St. Bernard case, the courts limited the enforceability of NFIP flood control measures to the claim the government can sue a local government on behalf of its policyholders (Herke 1993). FEMA and the DOJ were left with almost no judicial remedy for communities which fail to comply with flood mitigation requirements.

2.1.5 The Willingness-to-Pay for Flood Insurance

When voluntarily purchasing insurance, a policyholder implicitly evaluates their risk tolerance. However, many of the NFIP policyholders do not voluntarily purchase insurance in the traditional sense. Rather, policyholders are required to purchase the insurance as a condition to obtain certain mortgages under the Flood Disaster Protection Act of 1973 (FDPA). Lenders may also require flood insurance for mortgagees beyond the legal requirements. Policyholders are not entering into the purchase freely because they are a requirement for another transaction. Policyholders voluntarily choosing to purchase flood insurance are placing a type of bet on the likelihood of an event related loss, independent of other purchases.

In the case of the NFIP, the policyholder is betting that their expected losses due to flood and the value of reduced uncertainty are greater than the amount they will pay in policy premiums during the policy lifetime. A non-policyholder is betting that expected losses and value of reduced uncertainty due to flood will be less than the amount paid in policy premiums over the policy lifetime. In both situations, neither party knows the outcome a priori but both have the opportunity to evaluate the relative risk. The betting analogy lends itself to understanding risk tolerance (Nicholson 2004, 539–41).

Suppose a potential policyholder may purchase actuarially fair insurance, meaning the expected net pay-off is zero. If the policy is actuarially fair, a policyholder can pay a smaller amount in premiums regularly and will have a large loss compensated by the insurance policy. A non-policyholder would make no smaller payments, but have no recourse for sudden or large losses, either. However, if the insurance policy is actuarially fair, the annual expected losses for both the insured and noninsured are identical and have an expected value of zero dollars. Insurance is the smoothing of income for the policyholder, because it creates a regular and predictable expected loss in the premium, reducing the loss variance over time (Boardman et al. 2010, 173).

For required participants, the premium is a fixed cost necessary to acquire property in the floodplain. Therefore, holding an insurance policy through the NFIP may provide some value, but does not necessarily equal or exceed the premium, calling into question empirical estimates of the willingness-to-pay (WTP) for flood insurance based on studies of policyholders who are required to purchase insurance. For the voluntary participants in the NFIP, the analysis above likely holds.

A 1997 study of homeowners in Nevada looked into the flood insurance decision process. The survey found among NFIP policyholders, the most important reason was the mortgage requirement, followed by actual concern about flood risk. Less than 10 % of policyholders mentioned the cost of insurance or the use of governmental aid (Yildirim 1997, 47). Survey respondents who were not NFIP policyholders gave reasons ranging from a lack of requirement for a mortgage and damage would not likely exceed the premium for insurance. Less than half of survey respondents who had previously endured a flood had purchased flood insurance (Yildirim 1997, 50). A similar study showed half of all NFIP participants terminated their insurance policies after 2 years (Michel-Kerjan et al. 2012).

Sociological factors also play a role in determining how individuals react to the option to purchase flood insurance. Early in the history of the NFIP, a researcher at Mississippi State University researched the differences in perception between flood losses and fire losses. Cheatham (1975) discovered in a survey of businessmen in Columbus, Mississippi, that flood damage is perceived to be less than a total loss and there tends to be advance warning of a pending flood hazard whereas fires are perceived as a total loss and occur spontaneously. In addition, "individual disasters like fire, theft, etc., do not qualify a business for federal disaster relief like natural disasters" (Cheatham 1975, 47). The differences in expectations between traditional insurable events and flood losses explain some of the reasons why individuals or homeowners may be less willing to purchase flood insurance when mortgage lenders do not require it.

Researchers also found experience with prior floods correlates positively with purchasing insurance through the NFIP. Moore and Cantrell (1976) found experience with Hurricane Agnes in 1972 increased the likelihood of community involvement in the NFIP through both floodplain management planning and NFIP adoption rates (Moore and Cantrell 1976). Experience with prior flood events remains a constant theme when studying NFIP adoption rates.

Federal law also provides disincentives to participate in the NFIP. In a 1994 law review article, Griffith (1994a) argues the Disaster Relief Act of 1974 (DRA), which gives the president power to declare federal disasters and disburse aid following such a declaration, provides a disincentive to potential NFIP participants. The author explains since individuals are permitted to use disaster assistance under the DRA multiple times without taking mitigation measures, the DRA provides the disaster aid which should be provided by the NFIP (local governments, however, must hold insurance policies when seeking subsequent aid under the DRA). The author also notes it is feasible for the DRA and NFIP programs to complement each other rather than working at cross purposes since, at the time of the article, 7 % of the US population lived on land declared on the floodplain while 90 % of all federally declared disasters were flood related.

2.1.6 Distributional Effects of Flood Insurance

Distributional factors come into play with the NFIP, as well. At the start of 2010, there were 8.6 million people living within the 100-year Coastal Flood Hazard Area (CFHA), which is the part of the SFHA subject to coastal flood risk as opposed to riverine flood risk, as established by the FIRM (Crowell et al. 2010). With such a large population subject to potential flood hazard, there is significant opportunity for the macrosociological effects of both the flood hazard and the NFIP to become apparent.

As previously shown, there is a subsidy granted to homeowners in communities choosing to participate in the NFIP. A study by Shilling et al. (1989) in the late 1980s studied the effects of wealth transfer through the NFIP (Shilling et al. 1989). Their research used data provided by the Multiple Listing Service (MLS)[1] to estimate the effects on property values of the availability of flood insurance. The data show two key results on wealth transfer patterns. First, a house sitting in a floodplain is estimated by Shilling et al. (1989) to sell at an 8 % discount compared to the same house not located in a floodplain. Where FEMA declares the floodplain to lie can directly influence the valuation of homes. Home purchasers might trade off risk for property character, such as purchasers who might seek waterfront property with a view knowing that there is an increased risk of flooding. A hypothetical home spared the SFHA declaration due to being just outside the floodplain area, though of only marginally lower risk than its immediate neighbor, is on average worth 8 % more than a comparable property on the floodplain.

Second, in 1987, there was a 4 billion dollar wealth transfer nationally in favor of NFIP policyholders through the NFIP (Shilling et al. 1989). The wealth transfer is worth approximately 2000 dollars per insured property when the homeowner is provided subsidized insurance. Homeowners paying actuarially sound rates for flood insurance through the NFIP can expect to repay their real losses through the premium. Homeowners with subsidized insurance through the NFIP pay less than their real losses, based on largely arbitrary standards. Since the Shilling study, there have been numerous changes to the NFIP, but the subsidy is still available to many policyholders through grandfathering and other limits placed on the NFIP by Congress.

[1]The MLS is a system for cataloging real estate available for sale.

Other studies of pricing models for homes located in floodplains tell a similar story. Kousky (2008) found homes within the 100-year floodplain around St. Louis were priced at a discount apparently reflective of the relative risk of flooding following the 1993 Midwest Floods. Since homes in the 500-year floodplain showed no discount reflective of risk, Kousky (2008) suggests the discount may stem from the insurance requirement imposed on homes within the 100-year floodplain by the NFIP. Regardless of the discount's cause, Kousky (2008) argues providing more information to purchasers gives home purchasers better pricing information and suggests FEMA's 100-year floodplain may not be accurate enough (Kousky 2008, 44–46). Other flood control measures can alter the value of a home. Holway and Burby (1990) found for vacant land protected by a flood control structure, such as a levee, the land value increased by almost 700 dollars per one thousand square feet of land (Holway and Burby 1990). The increase to vacant land values can drive up the value of a home as the cost of land under a structure can be a significant portion of housing costs (Sirmans et al. 2005). In addition, vacant lots which had experienced a flood during the 5 years prior to the study lost almost 300 dollars in valuation per one thousand square feet of land.

Flood events can also affect personal finances. Research conducted in 2005 reviewed 18 major hurricanes and tropical storms from 1983 through 2004 and determined personal bankruptcy filings increase almost 50 % more quickly in states which are directly damaged by hurricanes (Lawless 2005). Lawless found larger claims following a hurricane were correlated with a smaller increase in bankruptcy filings, though the analytical techniques used by Lawless were overly simplistic. Without greater information about the relationship between bankruptcy filers and flood insurance policyholders, it is not possible to draw firm conclusions.

Bin et al. (2011) studied the income and expenses of the NFIP and found the premium charged to policyholders is regressive, meaning amounts charged increased less than proportionally with policyholder income as policyholder income rose. In contrast, the amounts the NFIP paid on claims were progressive (Bin et al. 2011). The authors found neither the regressivity nor the progressivity extreme and, over time, the differences between the payments, premiums, and income smoothed. The results suggest the NFIP is not subject to distributional pressures and it may be considered fair to insurance participants from the standpoint of social inequality.

2.1.7 Recent Changes and the Future of Flood Protection

Because of the devastation of Hurricane Katrina in 2005 and Hurricane Sandy in 2012, the future of the NFIP has returned to the policy agenda. Several changes to the NFIP have occurred and more are under informal and formal consideration by Congress. In 2012, the Biggert-Waters Flood Insurance Reform Act of 2012 (BWFIRA) included substantial reforms to the NFIP and its administration (Orie 2013). The BWFIRA changes allow lenders to include NFIP premiums in mortgage escrow accounts and consolidate mitigation activities within FEMA. Including NFIP premiums in mortgage escrow accounts is meant to reduce the substantial historical rate of dropped coverage after initial purchase by giving mortgage lenders the ability to monitor coverage maintenance. Otherwise, the mortgage lender has no ability to ensure coverage continues. However, several changes can affect the economic effects of the NFIP. One change includes the removal of subsidies for certain properties developed before the FIRM. Other changes will require reform of the WYO program for insurers.

However, others suggest more work is necessary. A study conducted by Anderson considered the effects of development on floodplain management and recommended policies to improve floodplain development (Anderson 2006, 92–93). One suggestion was to require all property owners within the floodplain to purchase insurance through the NFIP, instead of just owners with a federally financed mortgage. Another suggestion was to set federal requirements on permissible uses for development on the floodplain. Finally, the author suggested an incentive scheme to guide state and local jurisdictions in implementing better floodplain management schemes.

In response to concerns about wind damage versus flood damage, a move to add wind damage coverage to the NFIP failed in 2008 when the Flood Insurance Reform and Modernization Act of 2008 (FIRMA) passed both houses of Congress but was vetoed by President George W. Bush. As illustrated by Horne (2006), separating wind damage from flood damage can be difficult or even arbitrary in some cases, so a joint insurance scheme does not seem unreasonable on its face. A further concern raised by Brown is the potential for political pressure to drive the price of wind insurance below actuarial rates, which would further push the NFIP into debt (Brown 2010a). There could be political effects if the NFIP adds to its borrowing and the NFIP fails to bring sufficient revenue to meet its obligations and losses. The NFIP may be unable to borrow from the US Treasury as the debt grows beyond its financial capacity to repay and may require a bailout by Congress to prevent a default.

2.2 Benefit–Cost Analysis Literature

2.2.1 Benefit–Cost Analysis and Policy Objectives

The benefit-cost analysis (BCA) perspective provides unique insights to a public policy question. In balancing both the economic and social effects of a program, BCA quantifies and measures the effects to determine whether the program has a net social benefit, given transparent but not universally agreed upon rules for aggregation. Put simply, BCA is a tool to determine if a program contributes more to society than the program costs. In the case of the NFIP, BCA is different from testing the original objective, reducing the burden on the federal budget caused by flood events. The economic and social effects measured allow a BCA to synthesize direct transfers, economic gains and losses caused by a program, and the value of social objectives which may be inherent in a program.

The consumer surplus is a key concept in benefit–cost analysis as it seeks to measure how much individuals value goods or services. However, it can be difficult to estimate the consumer surplus for the NFIP because there is no functioning private market for flood insurance and many NFIP participants are not voluntary. Many public policies provide public goods for which no functioning market exists. As a result, many analysts impute a consumer surplus for some goods based on information available in secondary markets or surveys of potential program participants. The consumer surplus is based on the WTP and the WTP is a variable figure, depending on who is paying, their perception of the perceived effect of a good, and whether there has been a recent effect (Freeman 1989). The consumer surplus for flood insurance is a challenge for the BCA practitioner who must find a reasonable approach to estimation. The consumer surplus is discussed in greater detail in Chaps. 3 and 4.

Another obstacle to BCA policy analysis is measuring the distributional effects of a policy or program. The default analysis of a BCA assumes that the costs and benefits attributed to all parties are treated equally (Office of Management and Budget 1992). However, distributional concerns are a major focus of public policy and the political process. Understanding effects is a key to understanding a program's effectiveness, because a program can affect different individuals identically, but have different net effects depending upon the person's socioeconomic class. Further, different effects derive from theoretical implications based on socioeconomic class and estimating effect weights for different socioeconomic classes is a politically charged question. While there are variety of approaches to weighting distributional effects, there is no universally accepted standard approach.

The two obstacles to the BCA process have a particular importance when measuring the costs and benefits associated with the NFIP. Estimating the consumer surplus for flood protection is a particular challenge as flood protection is required for some, and part of its purpose is to reduce ad hocpayments from the public budget. Additionally, there are disparate and diffuse effects of the program across many socioeconomic divisions. Both problems impede the successful completion of a BCA of the NFIP. Despite potential problems, a BCA of the NFIP will provide information useful for understanding how the NFIP operates, whom it affects, how they are affected, and how the NFIP might be changed to better serve society.

2.2.2 *Benefit–Cost Analysis of Flood Programs*

Flood risk measures are a natural application for BCA and the use of BCA is historically fitting. Congress first required the use of BCA when evaluating flood control projects by the United States Army Corps of Engineers (USACE) in the Flood Control Act of 1936 (FCA). Arnold (1988, 91) states "[t]he only limitations on federal flood control projects were that the economic benefits had to exceed the costs" other than other certain limitations on local support for the project. In the FCA, Congress required positive net benefits, though USACE had performed flood mitigation for more than a century at the time. The OMB requires a favorable

BCA of new economically significant federal rules, supported by presidential Executive Order 12866 (EO 12866) and reaffirmed by Executive Order 13563 (EO 13563). Pursuant to the requirements, FEMA requires new flood control efforts sponsored under the FMA be supported by a BCA conducted in accordance with OMB regulations. As a result, FMA projects have already been subject to a BCA. The guidance standards from the federal government are more complex for flood mitigation activities. A circular from Office of Management and Budget (1992, 4) sets the guidelines for federal BCA estimates, but specifically excludes water projects, which include flood mitigation projects developed under both FEMA and USACE. BCA for water projects are required to use separate guidelines developed by the United States Water Resources Council (WRC) (Water Resources Council 1983), a governmental advisory panel composed of several federal department heads.

The standards developed by the WRC focus on economic development, a goal consistent with the goals of the NFIP. Nevertheless, the WRC document only applies to USACE, the Bureau of Reclamation (BOR), Natural Resources Conservation Service (NRCS), and the Tennessee Valley Authority (TVA); FEMA is not covered by the WRC standards. The requirements and standards for BCA of flood mitigation projects change based on what agency is performing the analysis. Beginning in 2008, USACE began a comprehensive revision to water project assessment designed to provide principles and standards which can then be implemented by federal agencies in a mission-specific manner.

The National Academy of Science (NAS), through the National Research Council (NRC), has commented on the proposed revisions to BCA for water projects. In particular, the NAS has noted BCA is a required component of the decision-making framework but does not specify how it is to be used (National Research Council 2010, 12–13). The NAS further criticizes the implementation of BCA by USACE in noting that the revisions continue historical practices of assuming how to monetize benefits and costs and by miscounting certain zero-sum transfers as benefits accruing in favor of a project. NAS has previously challenged USACE on its implementation of BCA for water projects, going so far as to criticize its over-reliance on monetized benefits and costs and lack of its independent focus on social and environmental costs and benefits of USACE-managed projects (National Research Council 2004, 70–72).

There have been other attempts to estimate the value of flood protections through BCA independently of the FMA and USACE processes. Ramirez et al. (1988) analyzed the value of a flood control project in Rushford, Minnesota. The 1958 Flood Control Act authorized a flood control project in Rushford due to nearly annual flooding of two nearby rivers. The authors found the Rushford project suitable for an *ex post* BCA. Ramirez et al. (1988) discovered the *ex post* BCA flood benefits were higher than the *ex ante* BCA benefit estimates. According to the authors, the increase in *ex post* benefits was due to revised damage estimates available after economic growth within the subject community. The economic growth came after the original project estimates. Within their sensitivity analysis, the authors acknowledged the uncertainty surrounding community growth.

Through the American Institutes for Research (AIR) evaluation of the NFIP, Jones et al. (2006) used BCA to analyze the net social benefits (NSB) of the building standards component of the NFIP. The building standards component is a part of the requirements for participating communities and requires communities set building standards to be able to withstand a minor flood, with flood waters less than the 100-year flood, before participants in the community can join the insurance component. Jones et al. (2006) found buildings constructed to new NFIP-mandated standards reduced damages compared to pre-FIRM buildings and the benefits of meeting the new standards generally outweighed the costs on an individual building level (Jones et al. 2006, 89–90).

However, BCA is not necessarily the best option for analyzing the value of environmental programs. Yasui (2005) analyzed the traditional methodology of BCA with respect to risk management in the context of ecological regulatory decision-making. Yasui argues BCA presents minima and maxima from potential implementations of regulatory options without significantly considering points in between and Yasui also argues stakeholders with relatively small benefits or costs may be ignored from an analytical perspective. Though Yasui argues for alternative regulatory decision-making frameworks, Yasui actually points to more circumspect analysis within the BCA process, especially in the standing determination, where whose benefits and costs are counted in the analysis is decided.

Ultimately, the measure of risk is the combined effect of the probability that the event will occur and the damage likely to be caused by the event. With flood risk, both are difficult to estimate (Bouma et al. 2005). Flood probability stems from hydrological and other environmental factors. Bouma et al. point out that it is difficult to estimate flood risk "without some major flood to anchor their perceptions." On the other hand, it is very difficult to measure the socioeconomic value of the damage a flood can cause. Actual flood risk, a key component of any measure of the potential costs of a flood, can be very difficult to estimate.

The problems with measuring risk illustrate the problem of estimating the value of flood mitigation projects. A flood mitigation program will have diffuse effects, beyond the immediately protected homeowners (Brown et al. 2008). There will be costs imposed on local governments which gain or lose revenue and face expenditures, but are not faced with the major costs following a flood. There will also be effects on the property values depending on protection levels. The diffuse effects are difficult to identify because of their far-reaching effects, going beyond the analysis normally provided in an environmental effect assessment.

Brown et al. (2008) argues for a multidisciplinary approach to measuring the net benefits of a dam project and argues it is applicable to other flood control devices. A multidisciplinary approach agrees with the work of Godschalk et al. (2009) who, when looking at all FEMA disaster mitigation strategies, concluded that understanding broad social implications of a disaster was necessary and could include qualitative studies in addition to quantitative. Accordingly, a BCA incorporating sociological and political effects is the best methodological approach for analyzing the NFIP from the policymaker's perspective. The policymaker can determine the effects of the program not just on participants but also compared to the intended consequences, especially when a program was created to relieve the administrative and financial burden on certain named groups of program participants.

Godschalk et al. (2009) also found a larger analytical basis is necessary when looking at disaster mitigation. Geographic and temporal spreading allows risk to smooth through both space and time, creating more accurate averages for measuring risk. While there is some concentration of both participation and risk to the NFIP in Florida, the NFIP is accessible and required in some circumstances across the USA.

2.2.3 Distributional Analysis and Benefit–Cost Analysis

A key assumption in calculating the net benefits of a project using BCA is the Kaldor-Hicks criterion (Boardman et al. 2010, 32). Kaldor-Hicks presumes that an option is economically efficient if those who benefit could, in theory, compensate those who incur the costs of the policy change. However, the benefits and costs of a policy may distribute across society affecting different social or income groups in different ways based on certain characteristics. A change in distributional weights can change the outcome of a BCA.

Measuring effects by wealth or income is an aspect of modern applied BCA. Many believe a dollar is worth more to a person with lower wealth and income because of a greater value to purchase necessities whereas a wealthier person may save or spend on something beyond a basic expense. Others believe a dollar in the community has the same value regardless of the holder since it contributes the same amount to society. Differing viewpoints on equity complicate the practical application of BCA, with respect to how distributional analysis should be performed (Harberger 1978), but distributional analysis may be appropriate when costs or benefits are systematically allocated unevenly across society.

An example of this tension comes from health hazard research. Viscusi (2000) points out that "[m]ore affluent individuals will have a greater willingness to pay for protection" than individuals with lesser means (Viscusi 2000) since the WTP for a good or service also depends on the purchaser's budget constraint. However, the benefits of a program like the NFIP may be of greater value to policyholders less able to protect themselves. Because someone with lower income likely has a higher marginal utility of income, a dollar's worth of benefits may be of greater value to them. Distributionally weighted BCA attempts to capture the effect of variable marginal utility for income.

Farrow (2011) examined the requirements of OMB for distributional analysis in BCA and discovered OMB's requirements lack details and leave implementation to the analyst. In the course of study, Farrow provided simple recommendations for analysts including the use of a distributional sensitivity test when conducting BCA. The distributional sensitivity test, like other sensitivity tests, subjects the assumptions of the BCA to a range of values to determine how the net social value changes. Rather than adjusting an input, the distributional sensitivity test focuses on the effects' assessments by social group. Equity concerns, however, justify the use of distributionally weighted BCA by using weighted costs and benefits to distinctly value the effects on diverse groups with standing. Someone with greater wealth will receive less weight to a cost associated with purchasing food, for instance, since their needs will have already been met (Harberger 1978).

Despite the reasons for using a distributionally weighted analysis, selecting a distributional weightset is a complex and subjective process. Boardman et al. (2010, 497) explain the motivations behind distributional analysis suggest weighting based on marginal utility. However, it is not possible to capture the demand curve for every distinct individual and there is no agreement on the value of change in income for a good or service beyond "most persons would, perhaps, agree that the relation is positive and its magnitude is larger for low-income than for high-income persons." Therefore, an objective approach to weighting based on the individual marginal utility is not possible. Selection complexity opens the field for multiple potential weightsets and allocation methods.

One method might order groups by their respective incomes and relates to the Gini coefficient. The Gini coefficient represents the deviation from an exactly equal distribution of income among a population (Lambert 2001, 27–29). A group where all members received an equal income has a Gini coefficient of zero. The Gini coefficient increases as the disparity in income among members of the group increases. For instance, the counties of the USA could be ordered by their median incomes providing an income distribution curve by geography. This approximates a Lorentz curve for the United States. In general, the Gini coefficient is two times the area between the observed Lorenz curve for a given group and the curve representing perfect equality. For example, Fig. 2.1 shows an area shaded pink, which is the area between the line of equality and a hypothetical observed income distribution. The blue area in the plot is the area under the Lorenz curve. Given the relationship between the Gini coefficient and the Lorenz curve, and the existing selection of group ordering by average income, a weightset based on the Lorenz curve is possible. One such weightset, based on the work of Atkinson (1970), uses income to establish multiple tiers, such as quintile groups, and assigns each tier a weight. Quintile groups in the higher income tiers receive a lower weight, though weights remain non-negative.

As pointed out by Farrow (2011), estimates of the Atkinson inequality measure are produced by the United States Census Bureau (USCB). Generating weightsets based on Atkinson's work relies on establishing a value, ϵ, which defines an inequality aversion metric. For common values of $\epsilon = \{0.0, 0.25, 0.5, 0.75, 1.0\}$, weightsets are available which provide five weights for incomes grouped by quintile, which measures the aversion to income inequality. Changes in the value of ϵ can lead to dramatic differences in the income inequality measure for a given population, depending on how income is dispersed (Lambert 2001, 127–130). Therefore, it is reasonable to use multiple distributional weightsets as a part of sensitivity analysis (Boardman et al. 2010, 501).

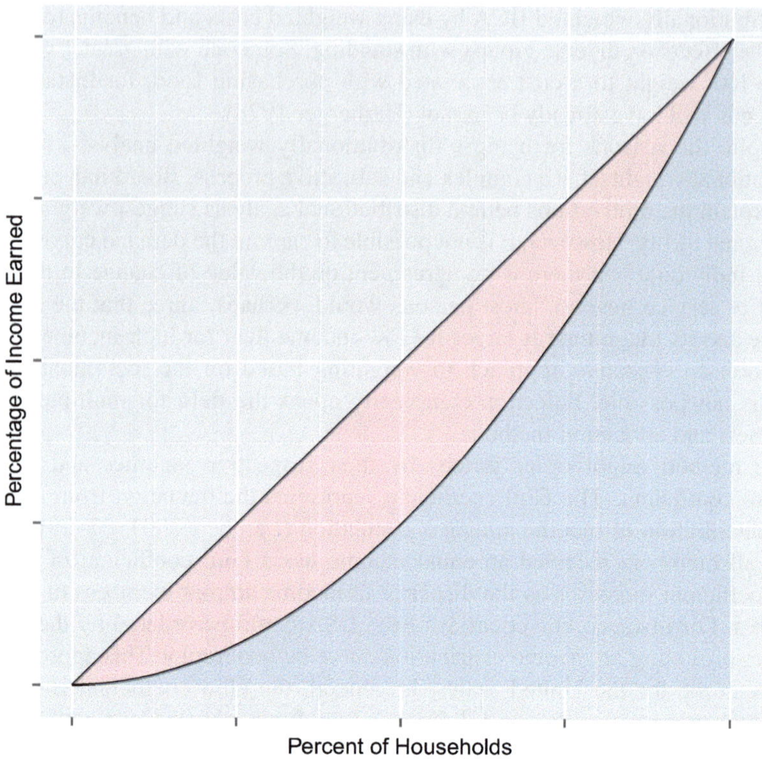

Fig. 2.1 Lorenz curve

2.2.4 Governmental Revenues

Government revenues are influenced by moving to a system where the beneficiary pays some or all of the costs associated with flooding. The NFIP reduces costs to the government and the general public (Sarmiento and Miller 2006, 65) because part of the flood recovery effort is prefunded by policyholders. After enacting the National Flood Insurance Act of 1968 (NFIA), Congress no longer needs to provide direct compensation to some affected individuals after a flood disaster. Further, because the funds for insurance come from a dedicated source, premiums, there is no burden on the general federal budget to provide compensation. The NFIP provides significant savings to taxpayers not affected by flooding. Because policyholders are unable to purchase flood insurance on the private market absent the NFIP, they either self-insure or gowithout. However, the NFIP is not a solution to government funding disaster relief directly from tax revenue. When a major disaster causes a shortfall, the NFIP is forced to use its credit line with the Treasury. Its borrowing capability, while constrained by Congress, does require the direct intervention of the government. A shortfall happens every 3–4 years, as documented by King (2005), and the NFIP has been in debt to the US Treasury ever since Katrina. Administering the NFIP through a separate fund allows for easy segregation of funds from tax revenues. However, the separate fund hides a large debt of the US government. Hurricane Sandy, which damaged the East and Northeast coasts in late 2012, has exacerbated the problem as the NFIP hit its debt ceiling before Congress raised the limit. This analysis will assume that there is no cost to financing the NFIP's borrowing, though this is a subject for further study.

The effects of the NFIP and FMA programs on government revenues can be considered a kind of distributional analysis focusing on the effects to government. Such an analysis would evaluate government income and expenses and determine, in a financial sense, how much money the government spends and saves due to the programs. A distributionally weighted analysis which only includes the costs and benefits to government would also answer the question of whether or not the programs have saved the government money, overall, one of the stated objectives of the programs.

In addition to the direct costs and revenues experienced by the government, taxation effects the broader economy, that is part of BCA (Hines 1999). The marginal excess tax burden (METB) is the deadweight loss to the economy caused by taxation (Boardman et al. 2010). The OMB justifies the METB on the basis that taxes "generally distort relative prices" causing a loss in welfare (Office of Management and Budget 1992, 13). In the general case, taxes distort the economy by changing the prices of goods and services away from equilibrium prices. This introduces a market inefficiency when the price changes. The inefficiency causes the market to purchase less of the good or service. Both consumers and producers directly or indirectly affected by the tax experience this loss. In the case of a tax on labor, such as an income tax, less is produced. Accordingly, there is a marginal decrease in the good service or labor produced and the effects of a tax can be measured through the METB.

OMB recommends using a fixed value of 25 % for public benefit projects (Office of Management and Budget 1992, 13). Other studies have suggested different values for the METB. Boardman et al. (2010) summarize several studies looking at the METB and claim for income tax funded projects, such as ad hocdisaster relief, the best estimate for the METB is 23 % with a range of 18–28 % (Boardman et al. 2010, 432–433).

2.3 Closing Remarks

The NFIP is a well-studied program with substantial economic effects. Many effects have a social dimension, where the effect has a different effect depending on the socioeconomic status of the recipient. BCA is a tool to analyze programs and can accommodate the complicated social analysis involved with the NFIP.

Chapter 3
Retrospective Analysis: Structure

This analysis uses benefit-cost analysis (BCA), to examine and value the effects of the National Flood Insurance Program (NFIP). The net social benefits (NSB) of a policy, the total benefits minus the total costs, is a monetary figure, usually measured in dollars. If the value is positive, there is a net social benefit to the program. If the value is negative, there is a net social cost to the program. The NSB of a policy can be compared to the status quo if not the current policy, other proposed policies, and against no alternative.

In practice, BCA is complex to implement due to the many assumptions necessary for a comprehensive and meaningful analysis. Determining whose benefits and costs to value can have political and empirical ramifications. Valuing effects, which may or may not occur directly in markets, stretches the limits of economics. Forecasting effects for a state of the world that does not exist can be difficult. Most analyses are open to critique based on the decisions made by the analyst, although guidance exists from federal agencies and professional practice to provide a set of standards for analysis (Boardman et al. 2010; Office of Management and Budget 2003). The results of an analyst's decisions can be tested through sensitivity analysis, which examines how the outcomes change for different inputs.

Before moving into the steps of the BCA process, it is necessary to define the characteristics of the NFIP to analyze. The BCA will consider the NFIP and Flood Mitigation Assistance (FMA) programs together, and produce a combined estimate of the NSB. Programmatic interdependence requires a combined analytical approach because the FMA program draws funding from the NFIP reserves. In exchange, property owners must live in communities meeting certain mitigation standards in order to purchase NFIP insurance and FMA program grants are used to meet mitigation standards.

The base case for the BCA will be the status quo of the NFIP program in place and operating as it did from 1996 through 2010. The alternative case considered is the hypothetical situation where the program did not exist and no comparable private flood insurance provider entered the market. It is extremely difficult to construct an

J. Howard, II, *Socioeconomic Effects of the National Flood Insurance Program*,
SpringerBriefs in Political Science, DOI 10.1007/978-3-319-29063-8_3

effective and accurate counterfactual for economic and policy analysis. This analysis is not an exception because the program has existed for several decades and the state of the world in its absence is not known. This analysis addresses the issue by capturing the differentials existing due to the program rather than directly measuring the total costs and benefits from each case. This analysis will find the NSB of the NFIP and FMA programs in 2010. In addition, the long-term NSB of the programs from 1996 to 2010 is calculated to 2060.

3.1 Research Question and Hypothesis

The primary research question of the BCA is whether the NFIP has provided a net benefit to society. With more than 40 years of history and the results and finances well documented, the experience with the NFIP can be measured quantitatively and BCA techniques can determine the net benefit to society to date. BCA provides several approaches to the question depending on how costs and benefits are assessed.

BCA is normally applied prospectively to evaluate a new potential program or change in an existing program. A prospective BCA will estimate forward-looking values for costs and benefits, discount future values, and provide a current year NSB. BCA can also be applied retrospectively to determine if an existing policy has yielded the intended effects. A retrospective analysis measures existing effects and values the effects. In addition, the process of discounting works to inflate prior years' spending versus later years, increasing the effect of earlier effects.

The first hypothesis examined will test whether the NFIP has provided NSB to society from 1996 through 2010. The hypothesis establishes a baseline for the NFIP analysis and provides context to other hypotheses. The period from 1996 through 2010 is due to the availability of data for both the NFIP and FMA programs. The period includes the extreme hurricane events of 2005, including Hurricane Katrina. Because of the severity of the 2005 hurricane season, a secondary analysis excluding 2005 will also be performed.

To consider this hypothesis, the NSB of the NFIP (the alternative hypothesis) are compared to a hypothetical situation where the NFIP did not exist and no comparable private program emerged (the null hypothesis). If the NSB of the NFIP are greater than zero (0), then the null hypothesis is rejected in favor of the alternative hypothesis. Formally stated, the null and alternative hypotheses are:

H_0: The net present value of the social benefits of the NFIP from 1996 through 2010 were less than or equal to zero (0).

H_1: The net present value of the social benefits of the NFIP from 1996 through 2010 were greater than zero (0).

3.2 Methodology

The NSB is the sum of the NSB of the NFIP and FMA programs. This analysis benefits from the recent research into the FMA program and adds to the literature by completing a new analysis of the insurance program. Where appropriate, the NSB of the NFIP and FMA programs will be calculated into the future. To start the analysis, it is necessary to establish which parties have standing to have their costs and benefits counted. The first is consumers, who purchase insurance through the NFIP. The second party is producers, who sell insurance plans on behalf of the NFIP. The third party is the federal government, which must manage the program. The final party is third parties affected broadly by externalities such as environmental effects of the program. The party definitions give rise to the social surplus model for the NFIP and mirror the analytic techniques of microeconomics.

3.2.1 *The National Flood Insurance Program*

3.2.1.1 A Social Surplus Model

BCA methodology normally defines the NSB in terms of total benefits less total costs. However, there is an alternative form that defines the NSB of the program as the sum of economic surpluses (Boardman et al. 2010, 62). Social surplus (*S*) is the sum of the consumer surplus (*C*), the producer surplus (*P*), government surplus (*G*), and the external surplus (*E*), each of which has its own definitional components to be discussed below,

$$S = C + P + G + E. \tag{3.1}$$

The analysis will use the social surplus method to find the NSB of the insurance program. Using the definition supplied in Eq. (3.1), the change in the social surplus, represented by ΔS, is

$$\Delta S = \Delta C + \Delta P + \Delta G + \Delta E. \tag{3.2}$$

From Eq. (3.2), it is possible to find the change in the NSB attributable to the NFIP versus an alternative where the NFIP does not exist.

3.2.1.2 Change in Consumer Surplus: ΔC

The consumer surplus measures the net benefit due to consumers from acquiring goods and services in the market. In general, the consumer surplus represents the net amount that consumers are willing to pay for a given good or service minus the actual price paid (Frank 2006, 160–162). The analysis assumes consumers would be unable to purchase flood insurance if the program did not exist, as was the case at the time the National Flood Insurance Act of 1968 (NFIA) was enacted. The base case, where the NFIP provides insurance to consumers, is represented by C^* and the alternative, where the NFIP no longer provides service, is represented by C'. Therefore, the total change in consumer surplus due to the NFIP is

$$\Delta C = C^* - C'. \tag{3.3}$$

In the event the NFIP does not exist, it is reasonable to assume the government would make payments to homeowners affected by flood disasters on an ad hocbasis as Congress did prior to the NFIA. Therefore, such ad hocaid is represented by a and

$$C' = a. \tag{3.4}$$

The consumer surplus due to the NFIP, C^*, includes the consumer surplus from program participants purchasing insurance, represented by w. In addition, in a retrospective analysis, consumers gain from any claims paid by the program to them following a disaster, which is represented by κ. However, consumers experience costs from the premiums paid to the NFIP as a part of the insurance program, represented by μ. If the program is actuarially fair and costless, then $\kappa = \mu$. The NFIP is not actuarially fair, especially among smaller subsets of policyholders. In addition, $\mu + w =$ WTP, where WTP is the willingness-to-pay (WTP) for flood insurance. The WTP here captures the entire area under the demand curve.

The model for the consumer surplus for the NFIP includes the direct benefits less the costs of insurance. The model includes the *ex ante* consumer surplus to be calculated in Chap. 4. The *ex ante* consumer surplus is often not included in retrospective analyses due to the belief that a simple accounting can accommodate any change in the consumer surplus. However, this analysis captures the value provided to consumers through the existence of the program, above and beyond the direct benefits of insurance claims. This *ex ante* benefit, looked at retrospectively, is described by Freeman (1989) and detailed in Sect. 2.2.1.

Therefore, the consumer surplus from the NFIP is

$$C^* = w + \kappa - \mu. \tag{3.5}$$

Substituting the equations for C^* and C' into Eq. (3.3) yields a final form for ΔC:

$$\Delta C = C^* - C' \tag{3.6}$$

$$= w + \kappa - \mu - a. \tag{3.7}$$

Equation (3.7) shows the complete change in the consumer surplus which is represented by the consumer surplus for flood insurance and the claims paid to consumers minus the premiums actually paid to the insurance fund and the estimated ad hocdisaster aid the government may sponsor.

3.2.1.3 Change in Producer Surplus: ΔP

The producer surplus measures the net benefit due to producers from providing goods and services to the market. The NFIP, however, is a government program and the program is managed through a dedicated fund, the National Flood Insurance Fund (NFIF). Accordingly, the main producer is better considered as a part of the government surplus, below. However, general insurance companies do benefit under the terms of the Write Your Own (WYO) program and it is appropriate to consider insurance companies' benefits and costs as a part of the producer surplus. The base case, where the NFIP provides insurance to consumers, is represented by P^*. The alternative, where the NFIP did not provide insurance, is represented by P'. The total change in producer surplus due to the NFIP is

$$\Delta P = P^* - P'. \tag{3.8}$$

If the NFIP did not exist, and assuming no producer would enter a hypothetical open market for flood insurance, no economic activity would take place regard to producers. The assumption is reasonable since the NFIP was created because there was no private flood insurance market, not to supplant an existing market. Therefore, $P' = 0$. In the case where the NFIP is extant and being serviced by individual insurance companies, a simple multiplier (φ) is applied to the value μ to capture the gross fees paid to industry through the WYO program. However, the payment from consumers, through the government, is a simple fee for the service of administering the NFIP. The fee allowance is designed to cover the expense of writing policies and processing claims. Administering the NFIP is assumed not to be a profit-making activity on the part of insurance companies and is assumed to be a pure economic cost to producers and is simply paid for by the government. So the amount of the WYO fees is subtracted back out. The base case estimate for the change in producer surplus is then zero, although the sensitivity of the results to the assumption will be investigated. Using the fee assumptions for the producer surpluses in each case leads to an estimate for the net change in the producer surplus due to the NFIP:

$$\Delta P = P^* - P' = 0 - 0 = 0. \tag{3.9}$$

3.2.1.4 Change in Government Surplus: ΔG

The government surplus measures the benefits and costs due to the government as part of a policy change. The government of the USA , through the NFIF, sees inflows and outflows directly stemming from the program. The base case, where the NFIP provides insurance to consumers, is represented by G^* and the alternative, where the NFIP does not provide service, is represented by G'. Accordingly, the total change in the government surplus due to the NFIP is

$$\Delta G = G^* - G'. \tag{3.10}$$

While the government did routinely provide disaster assistance to flood victims prior to the enactment of the NFIA, assistance was provided on an ad hocbasis and was not guaranteed to disaster victims as each round of assistance required an act of Congress, as described in Chap. 2. In addition, the government provided financial support to victims of Hurricane Katrina beyond repaying flood insurance claims. When the NFIP has not been sufficient to recover from a major flood, Congress and executive branch agencies have established other programs to support flood recovery. The analysis assumes the government would compensate the victims of flooding in the absence of the NFIP. Because of the assumption, per C', the government surplus must balance against the case where the NFIP did not exist. Therefore, $G' = -a$.

In the existing case of the NFIP, represented by G^*, government experiences inflows in the form of premium payments from program participants, μ. The government experiences outflows from claims payments made to policyholders after a flood event, κ, and due to the administrative fees paid to insurance providers, $\varphi\mu$, where φ is the percentage of the premiums paid as administrative fees. The government also experiences outflows, ζ, due to the expense of administering the program through administrative expenses separate from administering individual accounts, which are handled by insurance companies. Therefore, $G^* = \mu - \kappa - \varphi\mu - \zeta$ and the equation for the net change in the government surplus is

$$\Delta G = G^* - G' \tag{3.11}$$

$$= (\mu - \kappa - \varphi\mu - \zeta) - (-a) \tag{3.12}$$

$$= \mu - \kappa - \varphi\mu - \zeta + a. \tag{3.13}$$

3.2.1.5 Change in External Surplus: ΔE

Finally, the external surplus is the sum of benefits and costs due to third parties caused by the actions of consumers, producers, and the government. Like the other surpluses, the change in external surplus is the difference between the external surplus with the NFIP, E^*, and the case where the NFIP did not exist, E':

$$\Delta E = E^* - E'. \tag{3.14}$$

In the case where the NFIP does not exist, there are no external effects directly on consumers and producers, per the above analysis. However, the federal government is likely to give disaster relief aid and may cause some beneficiaries to rebuild in environmentally sensitive areas, which some consider an external effect. Therefore, the ecological effect, β, must be accounted for.

In addition, there is the externality of the effect of taxation required to pay for ad hocpayments in G'. The marginal excess tax burden (METB) is the effect on the economy from raising taxes to pay for government services, as described in Sect. 2.2.4. The METB is a multiplier, m, against the tax revenue to pay for the ad hocpayments, a. Accordingly,

$$E' = \beta - ma. \tag{3.15}$$

In the case where the NFIP does exist, the interactions are more complex. There is an externality of the effect of taxation necessary to fund the management costs of the NFIP, which is not paid for by NFIP premiums. By separating the effect of taxation from the government surplus, the government surplus estimate can be used to find the change in government revenues.

The effect of taxation is again represented by the METB, m, which is multiplied by ζ to capture the effect of taxation. There is also a potential environmental effect of the NFIP funding by rebuilding in potentially environmentally sensitive areas and there is ongoing debate about whether the existence of the NFIP may create inefficient use of the floodplain. The ecological effect, B, must also be accounted for. It is possible that other externalities exist due to redeveloping in flooded areas. However, neither potential effect is documented and given the data available from Federal Emergency Management Agency (FEMA) regarding the NFIP, it is not currently possible to identify and estimate them. Therefore, this analysis will not include them. Accordingly, $E^* = B - m\zeta$ and

$$\Delta E = E^* - E' \tag{3.16}$$

$$= (B - m\zeta) - (\beta - ma) \tag{3.17}$$

$$= B - m\zeta - \beta + ma. \tag{3.18}$$

3.2.1.6 Change in Social Surplus: ΔS

Using Eq. (3.2), the consumer, producer, government, and external surplus estimates are combined to provide the net social surplus given by the NFIP is, as a reduced form model,

$$\Delta S = \Delta C + \Delta P + \Delta G + \Delta E \tag{3.19}$$

$$= (w + \kappa - \mu - a) + (\mu - \kappa - \varphi\mu - \zeta + a) + (B - m\zeta - \beta + ma) \tag{3.20}$$

$$= w + B - m\zeta - \beta - \varphi\mu - \zeta + ma. \tag{3.21}$$

Consequently, the reduced form model is an attempt to find a sufficient statistic for the NFIP's insurance component (Chetty 2009) and starting point to more complex analyses of the NFIP. For better understanding, the features of the sufficient statistic and the key reductions are described as a ledger in Table 3.2.

3.2.1.7 Decomposition of the Social Surplus Model

Beginning with Eq. (3.21), several variables must be further resolved to calculate the net social surplus for the insurance component of the NFIP. As will be shown in Chap. 4, the expected consumer surplus for flood insurance is estimated to be 791 dollars per NFIP policy per year in 2010 dollars and is denoted by γ. It is possible to estimate the total consumer surplus earned through the NFIP because the total consumer surplus is the consumer surplus for flood insurance times the total number of flood insurance policies in force. Therefore, for an annual consumer surplus, w, γ is multiplied by the number of insurance policies through the NFIP, λ:

$$w = \gamma\lambda. \tag{3.22}$$

The placeholder for ad hocdisaster aid, a, must also be estimated. The analysis presumes the government would offer grants and other private relief directly to flood victims, similar to the government's response to flood events before enacting the NFIA. The placeholder estimate aligns with the original goal behind the NFIA, as described in Chap. 2, of transferring some of the risks from flood disaster to property owners more likely to be the beneficiaries of disaster relief. It is reasonable to assume ad hocdisaster aid would continue in the absence of the NFIP. Since the NFIP was designed to supplant a portion of disaster aid, it is reasonable to assume the ad hocdisaster aid to NFIP recipients would be equivalent to the payments made under the NFIP. Therefore, the expected ad hocdisaster aid for flood victims, in the absence of the NFIP, is likely equal to the claims against the NFIP under the program. Mathematically, $a = \kappa$ is used as the estimate for ad hocdisaster aid.

Finally, it is necessary to estimate B and β, the ecological effects in the external surplus. As explained in Sect. 2.1.4, environmentalists might argue the NFIP causes ecological damage by encouraging rebuilding on the floodplain. The ecological effects include the costs and damage to the environment from building in potentially sensitive areas. The estimated damage could also include the risk of future damage caused by not using land for mitigation purposes as well as any potential future risk to the rebuilt structure, itself. The effects may be far ranging and span long time periods. Accordingly, the ecological costs can be difficult to model and the full effects might not be quantifiable within the limited time periods for which data is available. Most of this cost is due to the lost capacity of floodplains to protect other areas against flooding.

As noted in the above discussion of ad hocaid, the government is presumed to give aid equivalent to claims made against the NFIP if the program did not exist. Accordingly there is some ecological cost that would accompany those payments, due to the environmental effects whatever spending accompanying those payments entailed. The ecological effects in both cases are poorly understood quantitatively and, therefore, difficult to value. There is evidence to suggest there is a net negative ecological benefit from the NFIP. This is based on broad assumptions about the value of ecological benefits and the net changes in development. Therefore,

Table 3.1 Variable list included in social surplus

Variable	Description
a	Amount of ad hocdisaster aid payments
B	Environmental externalities due to the program
β	Environmental externalities due to ad hocpayments
C	Consumer surplus
κ	Claims made against the NFIP
E	External surplus
G	Government surplus
φ	WYO fees percentage to insurers
γ	The consumer surplus for flood insurance, per policy
m	The METB
P	Producer surplus
μ	Premiums paid to the NFIP
R	The BCR for the FMA
S	Net social surplus
w	The consumer surplus for flood insurance
ζ	Cost of managing program to government

while the evidence suggests that $B - \beta < 0$, the actual value of $B - \beta$ cannot be estimated quantitatively. Therefore, these terms are assumed equal in the social surplus model.

Using the data available from the NFIP and the information above, Eq. (3.21) then reduces to

$$\Delta S = w + B - m\zeta - \beta - \varphi\mu - \zeta + ma \tag{3.23}$$

$$= \gamma\lambda - \varphi\mu - \zeta - m\zeta + m\kappa. \tag{3.24}$$

Relying on the analytical assumptions, the broad economic model, including some variables which cannot be estimated, is reduced to a final form using six variables with estimates readily available from NFIP financial data, the literature through benefits transfer (Desvousges et al. 1998), or through new primary research on the consumer surplus for the NFIP. These variables will be outlined in the following section (Table 3.1).

Because information on premiums and claims are available at the state and county level from FEMA, analytical granularity can be reduced from the national level to the state and county levels. Local data encourages jurisdictional level analysis of distributional effects of the program. In addition, by relaxing the assumptions made in the model, such as estimates of the consumer surplus for flood insurance, the producer surplus, or the METB, it is possible to perform break-even analysis, adapt other estimates of the values to the model, or search for optimal values through Monte Carlo simulation (MCS). Finally, this model forms the basis for analyzing proposed changes to the NFIP or new disaster insurance programs.

Table 3.2 Key features of the sufficient statistic

	With NFIP		Without NFIP	
	Benefits	Costs	Benefits	Costs
Consumer surplus				
Consumer surplus for flood insurance	w			
Payments for claims	κ			
Premium payments		μ		
Ad hocdisaster relief grant			a	
Alternative summary	$w+\kappa-\mu$		a	
Change in consumer surplus	$w+\kappa-\mu-a$			
Producer surplus				
Administrative fees to insurers (at rate φ)	$\varphi\mu$			
Administrative costs to insurers		$\varphi\mu$		
Alternative summary	$\varphi\mu-\varphi\mu=0$			
Change in producer surplus	0			
Government surplus				
Administrative fees to insurers		$\varphi\mu$		
Payments for claims		κ		
Premium payments	μ			
NFIP expenses		ζ		
Ad hocdisaster relief grant				a
Alternative summary	$\mu-\kappa-\varphi\mu-\zeta$		$-a$	
Change in government surplus	$\mu-\kappa-\varphi\mu-\zeta+a$			
External surplus				
Environmental benefits/costs		B	β	
Marginal tax burden (at rate m)		$m\zeta$		ma
Alternative summary	$B-m\zeta$		$\beta-ma$	
Change in external surplus	$B-m\zeta-\beta+ma$			
NFIP sufficient statistic	$w+B-m\zeta-\beta-\varphi\mu-\zeta+ma$			

3.2.1.8 Data Sources

Equation (3.24) includes six variables necessary for calculating the net change in social surplus due to the NFIP. Because the analysis is retrospective, actual figures for some of the variables can be extracted from the NFIP's financial information. FEMA provided data to the author (T. Scoville, personal communication, January 20, 2012), hereinafter called the FEMA Dataset. The FEMA Dataset consists of two components. The first component, FEMA Dataset A, is described in Table 3.3 and provides information on the number of policies, amount of coverage, and premiums paid. The second component, FEMA Dataset B, is described in Table 3.4, and provides information on claims and payments to policyholders. The FEMA Dataset is drawn directly from FEMA financial databases and as official government financial data are likely to be accurate. The dataset presumptively represents the entire universe of available data and is not a representative sample.

Table 3.3 Variable description for FEMA dataset A

Description
State name
A numerical identifier for the state
County name
A numerical identifier for the county
Year, 1978–2010 inclusive
Number of policies in force
Number of contracts in force
Amount of total covered exposure
Amount of premiums paid

Table 3.4 Variable description for FEMA dataset B

Description
State name
County name
Year, 1978–2010 inclusive
Total number of claims made
NFIF payments for property damage
NFIF payments for contents damage
NFIF payments for ICC

3.2.1.9 Adjustment to 2010 Present Value

Prior to using the data, it must first be adjusted to account for inflation and the time preference. This social discount function typically discounts later spending, providing a mechanism to track the assumption that something in the future is inherently worth less than the same thing today, a concept known as the time value of money. The social discount function also captures the opportunity cost of not using the money spent for some other worthwhile purpose. In a typical prospective BCA, the social discount rate (SDR) is applied to future years' net social benefits to provide the adjustment.

Because this analysis is a retrospective BCA, the SDR is applied backwards to older balances. This is because the investments made in prior years are presumed to have had an opportunity cost at the time and that opportunity cost is separate from inflation that may have occurred since the investment was made. In a prospective analysis, this is called the future value of money spent in current terms, and the future value is the inverse of the present value of future spending. In a retrospective analysis, the effect is to increase the value of money spent in prior years. Equivalently, the future value as of 2010 is computed for money spent in prior years.

Selecting an appropriate SDR is controversial because the SDR changes the relative weights of economic effects depending on when the effects are realized. For instance, a higher SDR reduces the relative value of long-term economic effects more than a lower SDR would. Boardman et al. (2010, Chap. 10) provides a number of options for a social discount rate. Options such as the marginal rate of return on private investment or the marginal rate of time preference are difficult to compute and are based on private consumption preferences. Boardman et al. (2010) also includes the expected governmental borrowing rate. There are some criticisms that the government borrowing rate may be upwardly biased. However, in a retrospective analysis, the government borrowing rate is easily observed and computationally simple. Accordingly, it is the preferred rate to use for the SDR in this analysis.

In a prospective analysis, the government borrowing rate is used by finding the average borrowing rate and subtracting the average inflation rate over prior periods to estimate the government's borrowing rate in real terms going forward. However, in a retrospective analysis, the process can be simplified to be based on actual government borrowing rate, which includes an allowance for inflationary effects, as the historical SDR on a year-over-year basis. This analysis uses the average constant maturity rate (CMR) for the 10-year Treasury bond for each year of the study period. This SDR closely aligns with advice from the Office of Management and Budget (OMB) on selecting an SDR for certain purposes (Office of Management and Budget 1992, Appendix C). However, rather than predicting or using OMB estimates for borrowing rates, this analysis benefits from the historical borrowing rates being observed and well known.

Additionally, because of the selection of an SDR rate based on nominal borrowing costs, the inflationary adjustment is not necessary. Borrowing rates are the combination of the expected inflationary rate and the social cost of capital. As a result, only one step is necessary to complete both adjustments. The values used in this analysis are provided in Appendix B.

3.2.1.10 Linking the Social Surplus Model to Data Fields

The variable λ is the number of flood insurance policies purchased through the NFIP. The value of λ is available from the NFIP dataset and is the policies in force for a given year. The values of p are given in Table 3.5 and a time-series plot is presented in Fig. 3.1. The plot shows a generally increasing number of policies with a sharp increase after 2005, possibly due to the effects of Hurricane Katrina.

The variable γ, representing the consumer surplus from the NFIP, is found in Chap. 4. The value is the consumer surplus per policy per year. The value of γ is 791 per policy, though the value is also subject to sensitivity analysis.

Using the same data as described in Table 3.4, the sum of the insurance claims provides the data for κ used in Eq. (3.24). The annualized amounts of claims are given in Table 3.5 and a time-series plot is presented in Fig. 3.2. The plot shows a generally increasing amount of claims paid over the study period and closely tracks the number of policies in force. The point in 2005 is an outlier on the plot, representing the claims due to the extreme flooding of Hurricane Katrina.

Data for the amount of payments is computed using the actual premiums paid to the NFIP during the analytical time frame. The amounts of the premiums are given in Table 3.5 and a time-series plot is presented in Fig. 3.3. The plot shows

Table 3.5 NFIP policies and premiums, nominal dollars

Year	Premiums	Policies	Claims
1996	1,275,142,562	3,693,018	827,788,942
1997	1,509,751,333	4,102,349	519,537,378
1998	1,668,235,535	4,235,117	886,210,419
1999	1,719,638,552	4,329,952	754,832,560
2000	1,723,812,790	4,369,074	251,720,536
2001	1,740,329,954	4,458,468	1,275,673,854
2002	1,802,277,733	4,519,798	432,350,618
2003	1,897,687,275	4,565,490	772,850,737
2004	2,040,786,564	4,667,376	2,220,079,025
2005	2,241,133,158	4,961,792	17,639,483,528
2006	2,604,712,840	5,514,675	638,772,642
2007	2,843,351,919	5,655,774	608,773,264
2008	3,066,725,391	5,684,268	3,415,230,017
2009	3,187,064,468	5,700,232	766,009,252
2010	3,353,755,725	5,646,726	758,008,836

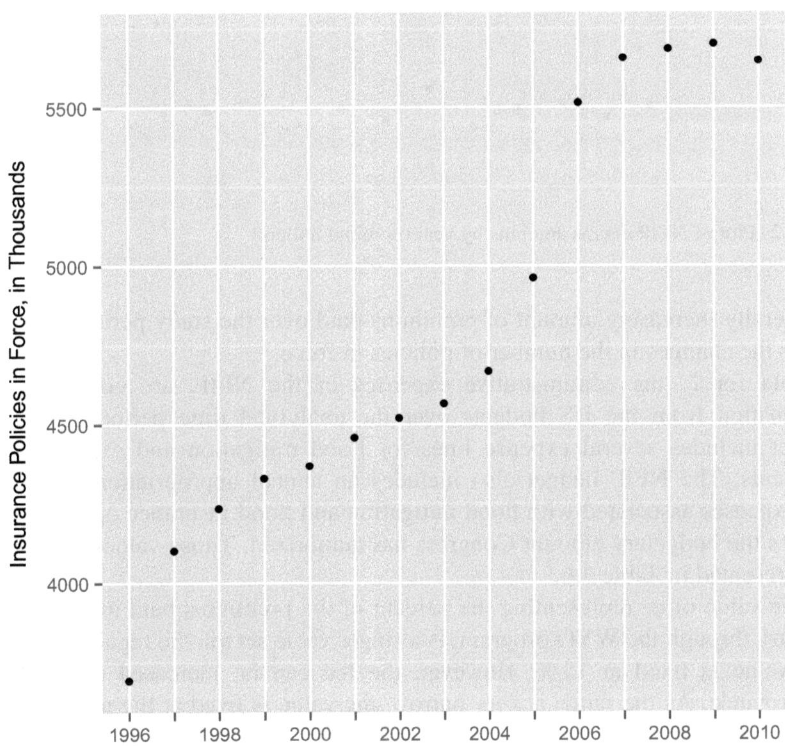

Fig. 3.1 Plot of NFIP policies by year

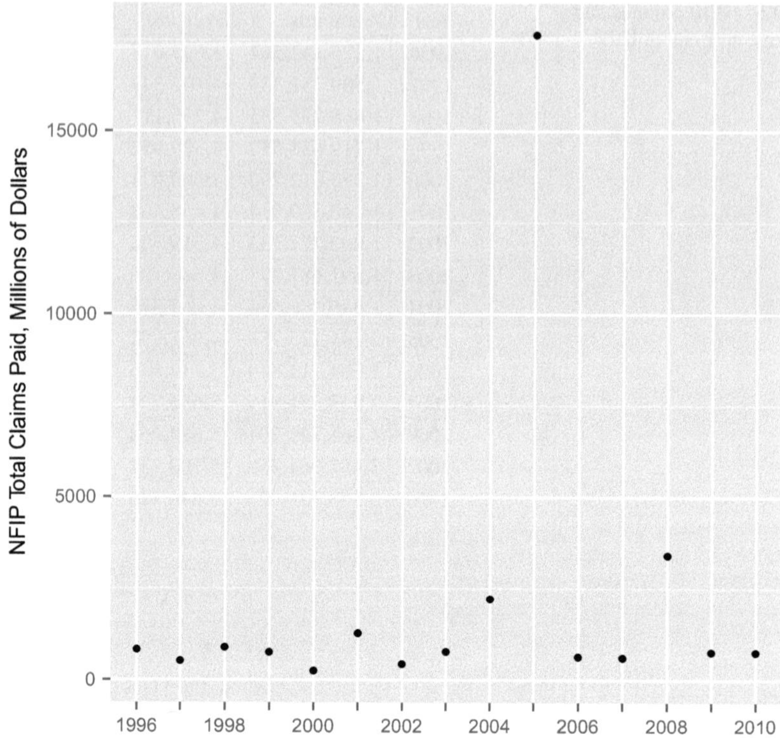

Fig. 3.2 Plot of NFIP claims amounts by year (nominal dollars)

a generally increasing amount of premiums paid over the study period and closely tracks the changes in the number of policies in force.

Data for ζ, the administrative expenses of the NFIP, are computed using information from the US budgets over the analytical time period. The NFIP's budget includes several expense lines for flood mitigation and expected claims payments. The NFIP budget also includes an annual appropriation "for salaries and expenses associated with flood mitigation and flood insurance operations" that defines the budgetary amount Congress has authorized. Those values are collected and presented in Table 3.6.

The value of φ, representing the percent of the premiums paid to the insurance industry through the WYO program, is a single value set via the regulatory process. The value is fixed at 15 %. However, the fee can be increased up to 2 % for performance. As the range is very narrow, the value is fixed at the midpoint, 16 % for this analysis.

Finally, data for m, representing the effects of the METB related to revenue for ad hocpayments in the absence of the NFIP, is a single value which can be derived from other sources. Because the NFIP is a federal project and given the OMB recommendation of 25 % is so close to the 23 % estimate of Boardman et al. (2010, 432–433), the 25 % value will be used for m. In addition, the OMB notes

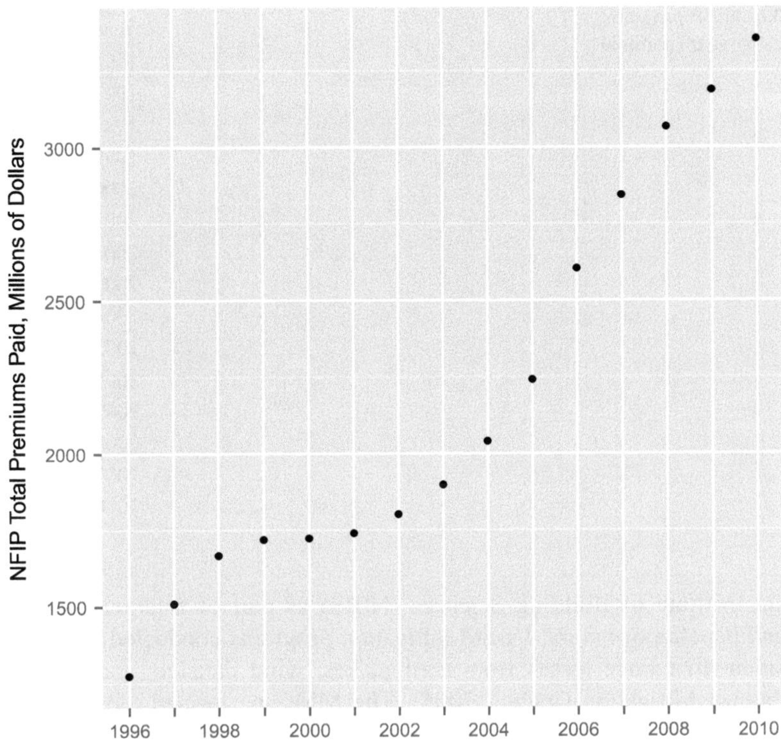

Fig. 3.3 Plot of NFIP premium amounts by year (nominal dollars)

that if there is a federal cost savings associated with the project, the METB can be reduced accordingly. The use of the METB in this analysis is in the specific case where there are no cost savings. Therefore, using the full value is appropriate. Other values will be tested through the sensitivity analysis, based on the recommended bounds of Boardman et al. (2010), of 18–28 %.

In this analysis, the METB applies to the deadweight loss incurred when the government uses taxes to pay for ad hocflood relief if the NFIP is not present and to the costs of administering the program if the NFIP does exist. Because of this, the METB for the costs of administering the program is subtracted from the NSB. However, the METB for the taxes paying for ad hocflood relief is not a deadweight loss if the NFIP does exist. Accordingly, that METB value is added to the NSB.

3.2.2 Flood Mitigation Activities

A BCA of the second part of the NFIP, the FMA program, is already available. It was completed in 2005 by the Multihazard Mitigation Council (MMC) at the

Table 3.6 NFIP program expenses by year (nominal dollars)

Year	Expenses
1996	20,562,000
1997	20,981,000
1998	21,610,000
1999	22,685,000
2000	24,333,000
2001	25,736,000
2002	28,798,000
2003	32,393,000
2004	32,663,000
2005	33,336,000
2006	36,496,000
2007	38,230,000
2008	45,642,000
2009	49,418,000
2010	52,149,000

National Institute of Building Sciences (NIBS) as part of a larger study on the costs and benefits of natural hazard mitigation programs conducted by the federal government to reduce losses from earthquakes, wind damage, and flood events (Multihazard Mitigation Council 2005). The MMC performed the review at the request of FEMA to quantify the future benefits of the three primary natural hazard mitigation programs conducted by FEMA. The FMA program is the flood mitigation program conducted by FEMA and was included in the MMC analysis.

In considering three mitigation programs, the MMC looked at both natural hazard mitigation programs and at building code improvements designed to reduce the effective damages from the hazard in question. However, with respect to flood events, the MMC only looked at mitigation programs designed to reduce flooding overall. In doing so, the MMC considered two types of flood mitigation. The first is project mitigation, which consists of grants used to pay for the reduction of risk in a particular site, often through a buyout system which dedicates formerly privately owned land to public use. The second is process mitigation, which may include the development of warning systems, advanced mitigation plans, and revised building codes.

3.2.2.1 Review of the Mitigation Grants Analysis

The BCA conducted by the MMC is a statistical analysis of more than 5000 flood mitigation projects funded through the FMA from 1993 through 2003. Projects, selected at random, were evaluated individually for costs and benefits. Using their results, the authors of the MMC report create an estimate of all FMA-funded projects' benefits and costs to create a net social benefit for the FMA program.

Several decisions made by the MMC report authors are notable when analyzing the results. The first is the costs of an individual flood mitigation project are estimated based on the grant size. This is a reasonable estimate as almost all costs associated with such a project are financial in nature and would be paid for using grant funds. When not the case, the authors adjusted the cost of a project to include other expenditures.

From an analytical perspective, the MMC uses the Hazus-MH modeling software produced under the direction of FEMA to estimate the benefits and costs of each of the projects in the sample space. The use of Hazus-MH is reasonable because the Hazus-MH software system is used to estimate the costs and benefits of individual flood mitigation projects as part of the proposal phase. However, the authors deviated from the Hazus-MH system in modeling the effect of businesses losses and other areas where the system was not sufficiently capable. The Hazus-MH software system was supplemented by additional analytical methods to accommodate certain externalities.

By using the Hazus-MH system, the authors of the MMC report do commit to using the datasets provided by FEMA for estimating both benefits and costs. However, the authors alleviate concerns about bias in the calculation process by conducting a number of case studies on randomly selected FMA projects to test their benefits and costs independently and use the information as an independent check on the integrity of the estimates provided through the Hazus-MH system.

An important result produced by the MMC authors using sensitivity analysis is discovering the NSB of a flood mitigation project is highly dependent upon the discount rate selected for future benefits. In their conclusion, the authors found a net social benefit of 11 billion dollars but with a high standard deviation of 3.8 billion dollars. The authors assumed a log-normal distribution of NSB and found there is greater than a 99 % probability the benefits exceed the costs for the entire FMA program. Overall, the analysis conducted by the MMC is sound and suitable for use in the context of benefits transfer, where the results of a BCA are included as a component in a separate BCA. Therefore, the conclusions of the MMC will be used to determine the NSB of the flood mitigation component of the FMA in this analysis.

3.2.2.2 Inclusion of the Mitigation Grants Analysis

This analysis incorporates the MMC study through benefits transfer. The authors of the MMC study create an estimate for the benefit–cost ratio, R, of the 50-year returns for the FMA process and project grants. The value will be incorporated in the final estimate of the NSB of the NFIP and FMA programs by using benefit–cost ratio and applying it to the FMA program data for the subject time period, using data provided by FEMA (Z. Usher, personal communication, December 5, 2011). This dataset, FEMA Dataset C, is described in Table 3.7.

FEMA Dataset C, like the other FEMA-provided datasets, is drawn directly from government financial databases and as official government financial data is likely

Table 3.7 Variable description for FEMA dataset C

Description
State name
County name
Grant recipient agency
Grant program, only FMA considered
Fiscal year of grant
Amount of grant

accurate. In addition to the estimate of the benefit–cost ratio, the authors of the MMC report provided a standard deviation for the estimate as well as a presumed distribution, log-normal. The distribution and standard deviation can be used to set the terms of the sensitivity analysis.

The benefit transfer will be made for each grant in the dataset separately using an annualized return rate for the 2010 estimate. The annualized return rate is calculated as the annual return rate necessary to achieve the benefit-cost ratio (BCR) R using the discount rate specified within the MMC study. Then, the return for each grant is calculated on a year-over-year basis. Finally, the amount of grants made in each year is subtracted from the annualized returns for each year. This process creates an FMA return amount for each year. That value is then socially discounted using the same social discount rates as used for the insurance data. For the long-term social benefits to 2060, each FMA grant value will be multiplied by the BCR value R, after the grant value has been socially discounted into 2010 values.

3.3 Sensitivity Analysis

The complexity of the NFIP and the FMA programs and their interactions suggest multiple sensitivity techniques. The techniques will include both naïve and sophisticated methods to check several of the analytical assumptions. The methods are outlined in Table 3.8. A distributionally weighted analysis, also a type of sensitivity analysis, will be considered separately in Chap. 6.

The first method used is a type of partial sensitivity analysis that eliminates values for the year 2005 from the analysis. Eliminating 2005 has the effect of eliminating Hurricanes Katrina and Rita from the analyzed record, which was a major event with an outsized effect on the NFIP and affected residents. The partial sensitivity analysis will show the effect a single large event can have on the NSB of the NFIP and FMA programs. Partial sensitivity analysis is also used to show the effect of the METB on the program.

Because each term in the analysis consists of a point estimate, there is a potential for statistical error to corrupt the final result. Sensitivity analysis provides an opportunity to analyze the errors involved and test the statistical assumptions included in the analysis. For this analysis, the sensitivity analysis will consist of a

Table 3.8 Sensitivity analysis methods to be included

Method	Comments
Partial sensitivity analysis	Elimination of 2005 from consideration
Partial sensitivity analysis	Elimination of the METB on ad hocrecovery funding from consideration
Partial sensitivity analysis	Elimination of the consumer surplus from the NFIP from consideration
Monte Carlo simulation	Stress testing of results to extreme values
Monte Carlo simulation	Stress testing of results to ad hocrecovery funding
Monte Carlo simulation	Stress testing of results to the producer surplus

stochastic simulation over the input variables to the models, also known as a Monte Carlo analysis (Boardman et al. 2010, 183–187). In addition to the MCS described in this section, it is useful to find the individual effects of the financial aspects of the programs, such as the effect of claims.

A final sensitivity analysis focusing on the distributional effects of the programs is not included here, but is described in Chaps. 6 and 7. It is not possible to eliminate the uncertainty inherent in BCA; however, the use of sensitivity analysis, specifically the use of stochastic simulation, provides a tool for understanding the uncertainty and its implications.

Chapter 4
Consumer Surplus of Flood Insurance

The consumer surplus is a fundamental building block of the social surplus as defined in Chap. 3. The consumer surplus depends on the willingness-to-pay (WTP) for a good or for a service. As described in Chap. 2, the WTP is the sum of the consumer surplus and any actual amount paid (Frank 2006, 160–164). The consumer surplus then is the benefit consumers receive for receiving something at a price less than they were willing to pay.

In the absence of a market, the consumer surplus for a good or service cannot be directly calculated. Estimating consumer surplus from the National Flood Insurance Program (NFIP) is further complicated by a legal framework that requires some policyholders to purchase insurance, regardless of the consumer's preference. Using estimated price data, the analysis will use a revealed preferences method (RPM) to estimate the consumer surplus for NFIP insurance. The analysis also uses some survey data, limited to background information capturing whether or not a respondent believes they are required to participate in the NFIP. Price information and actual preferences of survey respondents, such as whether they are NFIP policyholders, are obtained from the NFIP's financial records. The RPM methodology contrasts with contingent valuation method (CVM) studies, which normally ask if a participant would be willing to pay a certain amount (in closed-ended CVM) or how much they are willing to pay (in open-ended CVM) through a hypothetical questionnaire.

Price information, combined with insurance purchase information, increases the accuracy of the consumer surplus estimate. Respondents are unable to respond strategically and biases will not distort responses, because their purchase history is known. Due to the nature of the data collection, the analysis is closer to estimating the true consumer surplus by avoiding the complications arising from surveys addressing behavioral intentions through hypothetical questionnaires (Whitehead 2006). Limiting the model to voluntary policyholders controls for economic artifacts

J. Howard, II, *Socioeconomic Effects of the National Flood Insurance Program*, SpringerBriefs in Political Science, DOI 10.1007/978-3-319-29063-8_4

caused by the regulatory framework. However, this limitation omits some policyholders in high-risk areas where the policyholders presumably have a higher consumer surplus.

4.1 Model Description

The survey and financial data were analyzed using a Tobit model to estimate the consumer surplus for flood insurance. The Tobit model is a special case of a censored-outcome binary response model (Tobin 1958) where the response variable is bounded. In the case of an RPM estimation of a consumer surplus, neither the demand nor price paid can be below a lower bound of zero. Therefore, the Tobit model captures the censoring effect consistently whereas a purely linear demand model could estimate a negative demand for some market participants.

Haab and McConnell (2002) provide multiple methods for estimating a consumer surplus. In addition to the Tobit model, Haab and McConnell provided methods for demand estimations using Poisson models and negative binomial models. Both models are appropriate for outcomes that are count data. However, the Poisson model better represents a model where the mean and dispersion of the outcome are equal and the negative binomial model is suitable for overdispersed outcomes. The dataset includes a large number of responses censored at zero and the outcome is not a count, but a continuous price, measured in dollars.

The Tobit model has weaknesses necessary to understand for model selection. One weakness of the model is its reliance on the same inputs for both the demand level and participation outcomes. A model where different inputs describe the demand and participation, such as the Cragg model, overcomes this weakness. The Cragg model is a two-step model that uses a probit model to estimate participation and a Poisson model to estimate demand after participation is decided. The Cragg model is not used here due to its tendency to artificially increase the consumer surplus through the separation of analysis (Haab and McConnell 2002, 183–189). The Tobit model provides a balance fitting the estimation problem well and is appropriate for estimating the consumer surplus for flood insurance using the available dataset.

The analysis used a single data model estimated in two different iterations for different estimated flood insurance premiums as the exact premiums paid by respondents are not known. One insurance premium is for a high deductible plan and the second premium is for a low deductible plan, which is more frequently chosen by NFIP participants. Unlike Landry and Jahan-Parvar (2011), the model includes explanatory variables for the county in which the survey respondent's property is located, whether the respondent reported they believe they are required to carry flood insurance, as well as an indicator variable representing policyholders who are actually required to carry flood insurance by virtue of being located in the Special Flood Hazard Area (SFHA) and having a mortgage.

4.2 Data

The analysis used data collected by the H. J. Heinz III Center for Science, Economics, and the Environment in 1998 as part of a Federal Emergency Management Agency (FEMA) project to study erosion in the coastal zone (The Heinz Center 2000). The data was provided for this analysis by Craig E. Landry (personal communication, August 10, 2012). The dataset included both survey data and data collected from official databases and other sources. The survey was offered via mail to potential participants and the dataset consisted of 5,656 entries representing respondents across nine coastal counties, listed in Table 4.1, across the Mid-Atlantic, the Gulf Coast, and the southeast USA. The data collection targeted respondents owning property within 1000 feet of the coast, including both NFIP participants and nonparticipants. The selected survey respondents represent a broad sample of residential oceanfront properties. The Heinz Center collected data on property via local tax assessment records and combined the data with policy data from the FEMA and geographic data from geographic information systems (GIS). Finally, respondents filled out a mail questionnaire. The dataset includes observation weights reflecting the sampling structure. The sample did not include commercial properties. Statistical summaries of variables used are included in Table 4.2. The dataset includes a number of variables not used which are fully documented in other sources (Landry and Jahan-Parvar 2011; The Heinz Center 2000).

An important variable is the estimated flood insurance premium, if any, paid by a property owner. While the exact premium paid by a property owner is unknown, the premium can be estimated from property characteristics including value, flood zone, and coverage level. Because the policyholder-selected deductible and other elective policy features affect the premium paid, the dataset includes two variables representing the imputed lower and upper bounds, fpremlo and fpremhi, respectively. The variable fpremlo is the imputed premium for a high deductible plan and the variable fpremhi is the imputed premium for a low deductible plan. Landry and Jahan-Parvar (2011) note, based on research performed by Michel-Kerjan and Kousky (2010), most policyholders select the lower deductible level (500 dollars) suggesting the upper bound for premium level is likely to represent premiums paid

Table 4.1 Survey respondent count by county

County	n
Brazoria, Texas	487
Brevard, Florida	539
Brunswick, North Carolina	614
Dare, North Carolina	1060
Galveston, Texas	755
Georgetown, South Carolina	488
Glynn, Georgia	321
Lee, Florida	453
Sussex, Delaware	939
All	5656

Table 4.2 Summary statistics for variables used the NFIP consumer surplus model

Variable	Description	Units	Mean	Std. dev.
flcov	Amount of flood insurance coverage	100 dollars of coverage	737	879
fpremhi	Upper bound of estimated premium	price per unit of coverage	0.95	0.96
fpremlo	Lower bound of estimated premium	price per unit of coverage	0.81	0.84
incom	Reported income	dollars (thousands)	113	77
req	Imputed requirement for flood insurance	binomial	0.41	0.49
ocean	Binary variable for oceanfront status	binomial	0.43	0.49
vacant	Binary variable for vacancy status	binomial	0.54	0.5
subsidy	Binary variable for subsidy	binomial	0.56	0.5
azone	Binary variable for property in Zone A	binomial	0.43	0.5
vzone	Binary variable for property in Zone A	binomial	0.48	0.5
mort	Binary variable for property has a mortgage	binomial	0.45	0.5

by the policyholder. Consequently, the eventual base case analysis will use the higher premium-lower deductible model estimate of the consumer surplus as the typical value.

The dataset also includes a variable, flcov, representing the amount of flood insurance coverage purchased by a policyholder, in units of 100 dollars of insurance coverage, which is equivalent to the amount of insurance purchased divided by 100. The variable comes directly from the NFIP and is more reliable than data collected by a survey-based collection technique. The lower bound of zero dollars represents the case where no insurance is purchased. Therefore, 49.6 % of the survey respondents were nonparticipants in the NFIP. In addition, in 1998, the NFIP limited policyholders to a maximum of 250,000 dollars of coverage. Approximately 8.03 % of policyholders in the sample purchased the maximum coverage available. The program minimum (zero dollars) and maximum (250,000 dollars) effectively censor the dataset at both the left and right boundaries. The sample mean is a policy of 73,737 dollars with an estimated premium of 522 dollars for the policy using the high premium-low deductible estimate for the premium.

In addition to the economically imputed variables created by others, the use of additional variables simplifies the analysis. A binary variable, sfha, denotes whether a property is located in the SFHA. The sfha variable is true (1) if either azone or vzone is true (1). The variable azone is true if the property is located in NFIP Zone A, which is subject to inundation by the 100-year flood. The variable vzone is true if the property is located in NFIP Zone V representing coastal areas subject to inundation by the 100-year flood with special hazards due to storm surge waves.

A second binary variable, req, denotes whether or not NFIP coverage is required for the property. The req variable is true (1) if both sfha and mort are true (1), where mort is true if the survey respondent indicated they had a mortgage on the property. The assignment assumes all mortgages are subject to federal lending requirements for flood insurance, which is not necessarily the case. The req variable is distinct from the survey response variable, requ, representing whether or not a respondent believes they are required to carry flood insurance as part of their mortgage borrowing. Finally, a dummy variable, county, represents the county of the respondent, which is aggregated from the individual county indicator variables.

Other studies, beyond the original collection effort by The Heinz Center (2000), have used the survey data. Kriesel and Landry (2004) used the survey data in conjunction with FEMA information and other data sources to analyze NFIP participation rates in the coastal flood zone, notably finding the demand for flood insurance is inelastic with respect to price, due to the legal requirement for some policyholders to purchase insurance. Landry and Jahan-Parvar (2011) used the survey data to investigate determinants of coverage level via a Tobit model. They found flood insurance coverage increases with flood risk and with borrowing via a mortgage.

Importantly, the analysis will reduce the data to include only survey respondents who are not required to purchase flood insurance through the NFIP and who also do not believe they are required to purchase flood insurance through the NFIP to implement the analysis. Including only these respondents causes the model to estimate the behavior of respondents in the absence of the NFIP. The model will yield the best estimate for a mean national consumer surplus of the NFIP, by preventing policyholders who are forced into the program by federal law from artificially increasing the demand and consumer surplus for flood insurance at FEMA's premium rate.

This approach, however, may overstate the consumer surplus for flood insurance. While there are data for respondents who purchased flood insurance and respondents who did not purchase flood insurance, the data only includes respondents with property within 1000 feet of the coast. In effect, this approach uses voluntary flood insurance purchases not within a higher risk area to estimate the consumer surplus for those required to purchase insurance in higher risk areas. Accordingly, if the nonvoluntary policyholders would not purchase flood insurance if the requirement did not exist, the consumer surplus estimated will be larger than the actual value of the consumer surplus.

4.3 Estimation

Implicit in the methodological design is the assumption that flood insurance coverage purchased decreases as the price of insurance increases. The relationship, a standard demand model, is required for the Tobit method to estimate the consumer surplus correctly. Figure 4.1 shows the percent of voluntary participants willing

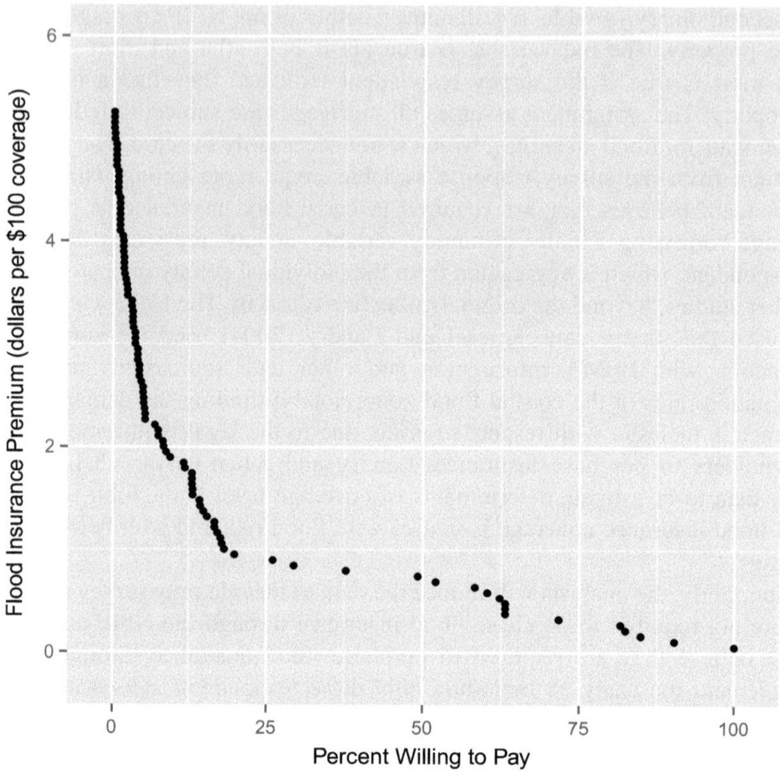

Fig. 4.1 Percent of voluntary purchasers by premium (upper bound of the insurance premium rate)

to purchase insurance at decreasing price levels, using the higher estimate for insurance premiums. Figure 4.2 provides the same plot for the lower estimate of the insurance premiums. Both figures show decreasing numbers of participants as the price of insurance increases.

Data with a lower bound is left-censored, with a lower bound of zero dollars of insurance purchased. However, the amount of flood insurance purchased by policyholders was limited to 250,000 dollars by FEMA regulations. The limit is observable in the dataset where the maximum observed value of the flood insurance coverage variable, flcov, is 2500, in units of 100 dollars of coverage. An upper bound is right-censoring. Because the data are also right-censored, it is necessary to use an implementation of the Tobit model accepting both right- and left-censoring.

In practice, the dependent variable, y_i, in the Tobit model is specified, like the ordinary least squares (OLS) model, as

$$y_i^* = \beta x_i + \mu_i, \tag{4.1}$$

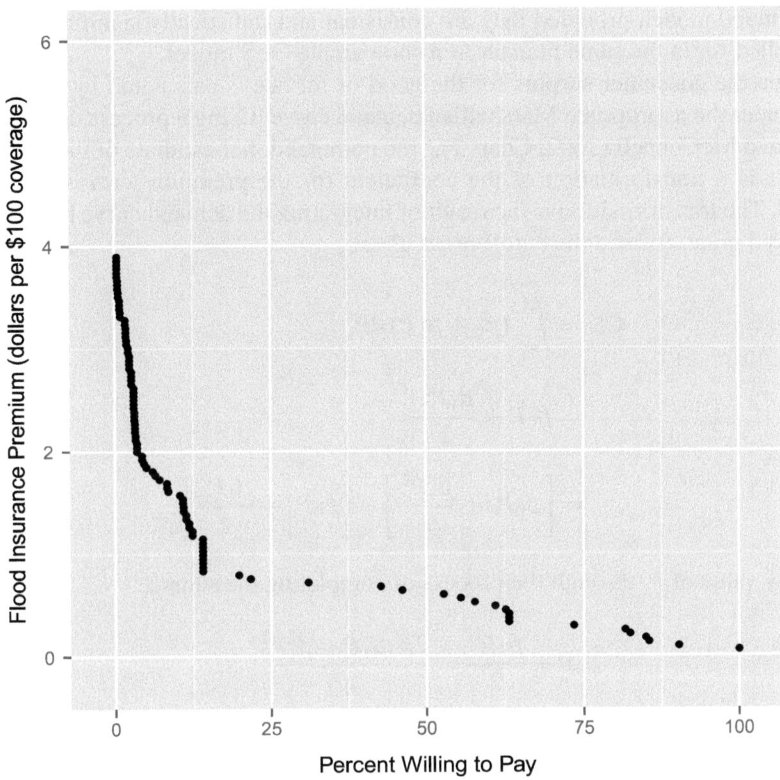

Fig. 4.2 Percent of voluntary purchasers by premium (lower bound of the insurance premium rate)

where μ_i is the unobserved error in the estimate and is presumed to be normally distributed and centered at 0. Unlike the OLS model, the dependent variable, y_i^*, is a latent and unobserved variable. Based on the results of the Tobit estimation procedure,

$$y_i = \begin{cases} y_i^*, & y_i^* > 0 \\ 0, & \text{otherwise} \end{cases}, \tag{4.2}$$

where y_i is the observed response variable. For example, suppose a demand model were estimated, using Tobit,

$$y = \beta_0 + \beta_1 x_1 + \cdots + \beta_n x_n + \epsilon, \tag{4.3}$$

where x_1 is the price per unit of the good or service, β_1 is the estimated coefficient of the price, and y is the amount purchased. Additional explanatory variables in the demand model, provided they are consistent and statistically significant, can be controlled for in the same manner as a comparable OLS model.

Then the consumer surplus for the good or service is calculated by finding the area under the appropriate Marshallian demand curve. Using a process described by Haab and McConnell (2002, Chap. 7),[1] the nominal dollar estimate of the consumer surplus is a transformation of the coefficient for the premium term of the Tobit model. The transformation is the result of integrating the demand curve between the observed price, P_0, and the cutoff price, P_c, so,

$$\mathrm{CS} = \int_{P_0}^{P_c} (\beta_0 + \beta_1 P)\, dP \tag{4.4}$$

$$= \beta_0 P + \frac{\beta_1 P^2}{2}\Bigg|_{P_0}^{P_c} \tag{4.5}$$

$$= \left[\beta_0 P_c + \frac{\beta_1 P_c^2}{2}\right] - \left[\beta_0 P_0 + \frac{\beta_1 P_0^2}{2}\right]. \tag{4.6}$$

For any value of P, through the process of completing the square,

$$\beta_0 P + \frac{\beta_1 P^2}{2} = \frac{2\beta_0\beta_1 P + \beta_1^2 P^2}{2\beta_1} \tag{4.7}$$

$$= \frac{(\beta_0 + \beta_1 P)^2}{2\beta_1} - \frac{(\beta_0)^2}{2\beta_1}. \tag{4.8}$$

Substituting the result of Eq. (4.8) into Eq. (4.6) yields

$$\left[\beta_0 P_c + \frac{\beta_1 P_c^2}{2}\right] - \left[\beta_0 P_0 + \frac{\beta_1 P_0^2}{2}\right]$$

$$= \left[\frac{(\beta_0 + \beta_1 P_c)^2}{2\beta_1} - \frac{(\beta_0)^2}{2\beta_1}\right] - \left[\frac{(\beta_0 + \beta_1 P_0)^2}{2\beta_1} - \frac{(\beta_0)^2}{2\beta_1}\right] \tag{4.9}$$

$$= \frac{(\beta_0 + \beta_1 P_c)^2}{2\beta_1} - \frac{(\beta_0 + \beta_1 P_0)^2}{2\beta_1}. \tag{4.10}$$

At the cutoff price, the demand is zero and $\beta_0 + \beta_1 P_c = 0$, by definition, since the cutoff price is the price at which there are no purchasers (Haab and McConnell 2002, 160–162). Similarly, the demand is y from Eq. (4.3) and $\beta_0 + \beta_1 P_c = y$. Therefore,

[1]Haab and McConnell (2002) use WTP and consumer surplus interchangeably due to the parameters of their example case, where the WTP and consumer surplus were equal. This is not generally true.

$$\frac{(\beta_0 + \beta_1 P_c)^2}{2\beta_1} - \frac{(\beta_0 + \beta_1 P_0)^2}{2\beta_1} = \frac{0^2}{2\beta_1} - \frac{y^2}{2\beta_1} \tag{4.11}$$

$$= -\frac{y^2}{2\beta_1}, \tag{4.12}$$

where y is the amount purchased and Eq. (4.12) is the consumer surplus (Bockstael et al. 1992; Hellerstein 1992). A linear specification is typically used given the intent of estimating the consumer surplus. Nonlinear specifications, such as quadratic specifications of the demand model, can lead to an estimated infinite consumer surplus if there is no choke price for which demand is zero. Other nonlinear specifications, such as logarithmic specifications, may not satisfy the expected requirements of a demand curve. Accordingly, this analysis uses a linear specification for the demand curve.

To calculate the consumer surplus on a per policy basis, the consumer surplus can be calculated for each customer for which there is information in the dataset and the results averaged across the dataset. Therefore, the mean consumer surplus is

$$-\frac{y^2}{2\beta_1} = \sum_{i=1}^{n} -\frac{y_i^{*2}}{2\beta_1}/n, \tag{4.13}$$

where n is the number of observations in the sample and y_i^* is the amount of the product purchased by the ith member of the sample.

To calculate using the estimated amount of the product purchased, $y_i^* = \hat{y}_i$, where $\hat{y}_i$ is the fitted estimated amount of the product purchased by the ith member of the sample. However, to estimate using the observed amount of the product purchased, $y_i^* = y_i$, where y_i is the actual amount of the product purchased. Using the observed amount of a product purchased usually leads to larger estimates of the consumer surplus. Haab and McConnell (2002, 163) suggest using the estimated amount of the product purchased when using Tobit to find the consumer surplus. The result of the consumer surplus is in dollars per consumer if the amount purchased is in units and the price is given in dollars per unit. The model is estimated on transformations of the y and x terms representing demand and price, respectively. In this analysis, the transformation from a standard demand model is the amount of insurance purchased divided by 100 and the price of insurance is multiplied by 100, a reciprocal transformation. The consumer surplus is invariant to the terms of expression for price and demand, provided the terms of expression are inverse to each other.

The result remains in dollars per consumer even if the amount purchased changes units, provided the price changes inversely. To find the consumer surplus of the NFIP, the product purchased is the amount of insurance purchased per policy and the result will be in dollars per policy. The data includes the amount of insurance purchased in units of 100 dollars of coverage. The price is given in dollars per 100 dollars of coverage.

4.4 Results

The model has been estimated with the R programming language using the *tobit()* function from the **AER** package (Kleiber and Zeileis 2008, 141–143). The Tobit implementation provided by *tobit()* is a maximum-likelihood estimation (MLE) method as described by Wooldridge (2010, 670–677). A complete listing of the model estimates is available in Table 4.3 for the higher premium estimate and Table 4.4 for the lower premium estimate.

In both estimates, all non-county identification variables are consistent and significant to at least $p < 0.05$. In general, the county indicator variable appears to capture local effects altering perceived risk with respect to flooding not captured through the actual risk embodied in the SFHA designation and implicitly in the estimated variable req. There is a strong negative coefficient for flood insurance premium price, the variable fprem, across flood insurance price pairings. For both estimates, the relationship is significant to $p < 0.001$. For instance, in the case of the

Table 4.3 Regression results for upper bound of premium estimate

	Non-required	Floodplain	All respondents
(Intercept)	−1842.98 (317.03)***	−1315.53 (208.65)***	−1593.38 (212.79)***
fprem	−564.95 (59.67)***	−454.64 (36.99)***	−465.31 (38.52)***
log(income)	574.22 (55.71)***	538.21 (37.06)***	575.95 (37.09)***
Brevard county	−853.53 (234.11)***	41.67 (165.40)	−662.90 (157.61)***
Brunswick county	369.15 (218.72)	591.30 (138.62)***	511.33 (145.58)***
Dare county	−153.98 (223.35)	174.78 (140.48)	135.23 (147.16)
Galveston county	−7.59 (218.27)	410.61 (138.41)**	334.88 (144.28)*
Georgetown county	1348.26 (265.65)***	1343.04 (162.42)***	1338.35 (171.76)***
Glynn county	102.61 (271.37)	568.78 (170.49)***	630.44 (177.82)***
Lee county	201.31 (259.88)	524.53 (159.76)**	501.10 (169.05)**
Sussex county	−445.61 (211.14)*	−121.52 (134.48)	−130.40 (141.94)
ocean	831.61 (90.35)***	581.53 (57.44)***	713.25 (57.67)***
vacant	−255.10 (92.78)**	−167.59 (61.60)**	−210.37 (61.74)***
subsidy	−530.15 (95.64)***	−765.98 (61.08)***	−677.95 (61.18)***
Log(scale)	7.40 (0.03)***	7.15 (0.02)***	7.21 (0.02)***
AIC	15502.85	27273.90	29192.28
BIC	15575.64	27354.18	29273.70
Log likelihood	−7736.43	−13621.95	−14581.14
Deviance	1130.84	1693.80	1831.98
Total	946	1559	1682
Left-censored	222	197	244
Uncensored	601	1117	1177
Right-censored	123	245	261
Wald Test	475.87	1010.59	1086.55

$^{***}p < 0.001$, $^{**}p < 0.01$, $^{*}p < 0.05$

Table 4.4 Regression results for lower bound of premium estimate

	Non − required	Floodplain	All respondents
(Intercept)	−1503.55 (311.15)***	−1146.40 (204.96)***	−1356.00 (208.95)***
fprem	−1032.06 (84.75)***	−772.69 (50.94)***	−835.88 (53.74)***
log(income)	568.45 (54.72)***	530.47 (36.54)***	568.98 (36.47)***
Brevard county	−1040.19 (231.20)***	−100.08 (163.54)	−792.92 (155.36)***
Brunswick county	275.89 (217.83)	549.76 (137.90)***	450.40 (144.64)**
Dare county	−400.65 (221.75)	41.71 (139.11)	−43.91 (145.66)
Galveston county	−36.20 (217.01)	404.80 (137.55)**	306.06 (143.06)*
Georgetown county	1105.89 (262.08)***	1208.73 (160.58)***	1174.28 (169.50)***
Glynn county	−178.29 (268.82)	392.71 (168.89)*	413.99 (175.91)*
Lee county	−41.16 (257.10)	371.88 (158.22)*	311.32 (167.15)
Sussex county	−647.38 (209.96)**	−238.05 (133.43)	−279.13 (140.70)*
Ocean	787.84 (88.75)***	557.31 (56.66)***	687.84 (56.71)***
Vacant	−191.04 (91.51)*	−121.90 (60.99)*	−160.55 (60.99)**
Subsidy	−364.48 (93.18)***	−598.76 (59.61)***	−526.34 (59.59)***
Log(scale)	7.37 (0.03)***	7.13 (0.02)***	7.19 (0.02)***
AIC	15415.52	27167.38	29063.84
BIC	15488.30	27247.66	29145.25
Log likelihood	−7692.76	−13568.69	−14516.92
Deviance	1115.91	1693.93	1829.84
Total	946	1559	1682
Left-censored	222	197	244
Uncensored	601	1117	1177
Right-censored	123	245	261
Wald Test	514.95	1062.51	1152.32

$^{***}p < 0.001$, $^{**}p < 0.01$, $^{*}p < 0.05$

higher premium model, for every one cent (0.01 dollars) increase in the price of 100 dollars of insurance, there is a −465.31 dollar decrease in the amount of insurance purchased. In addition to the model estimates for those not required to purchase flood insurance, Tables 4.3 and 4.4 include model estimates for survey respondents located on the floodplain and for all survey respondents.

The finding reflects the classic demand curve expectation of an inverse relationship between the price of a product and the quantity demanded. The finding also agrees with the findings of Landry and Jahan-Parvar (2011) reporting a negative relationship across different subsidy groupings. The variable subsidy is an indicator variable representing whether or not the policyholder is eligible for an insurance subsidy due to being built before Flood Disaster Protection Act of 1973 (FDPA). The subsidy variable has a positive coefficient and captures the effects the discounts can have on the consumer surplus. The ocean variable, an indicator variable for whether the property is oceanfront, and the variable vacant, capturing whether the property is occupied, were both significant, as well.

To estimate the total consumer surplus per policyholder, the fitted outcomes of the model are estimated and the consumer surplus is calculated for each survey respondent. If an individual respondent's fitted estimate is a negative insurance purchase, the amount purchased is reset to 0. Then the consumer surplus is calculated using Eq. (4.12). The average consumer surplus is the mean of the individual respondent's consumer surpluses. Accordingly, for the high estimated insurance premium, using Eq. (4.13), where y_i is the estimated amount of insurance purchased from the fitted estimates, the consumer surplus in dollars per policy is

$$\mathrm{CS}_H = \sum_{i=1}^{n} -\frac{y_i^{*2}}{2\beta_1}/n = \sum_{i=1}^{n} -\frac{\hat{y}_i^2}{2\beta_1}/n = 591, \tag{4.14}$$

in 1998 dollars per policy. For comparison, the mean premium per year is 522 dollars and the consumer surplus is approximately 113 % of the premium. In 2010 dollars, $\mathrm{CS}_H = 791$.

It is also possible to estimate the consumer surplus using the observed insurance demand instead of the fitted estimate for purchases. In this case, the consumer surplus is estimated using Eq. (4.13) where y_i is the observed amount of insurance purchased. Again, the consumer surplus is estimated for each survey respondent and the average consumer surplus is calculated. The process is replicated for the lower bound of the insurance premium rate and again replicated for the model where the estimates are based only on those survey respondents with properties located on the floodplain and for all survey respondents, regardless of where their property is located. The results for all cases of the higher-bound of the premium estimate are included in Table 4.5 and the estimates for all cases with the lower-bound premium estimate are included in Table 4.6.

These results show an increasing consumer surplus as the number of respondents required to purchase insurance increases. Regardless of which premium is selected or how the mean consumer surplus is calculated, the lowest consumer surplus is for the group of voluntary purchasers. The second lowest consumer surplus is estimated for all respondents. Finally, the largest consumer surplus is estimated for respondents with properties located on the floodplain. The increasing surplus can stem from two potential sources.

Table 4.5 Estimates of the consumer surplus for flood insurance, high premium (dollars per policy)

	Non-required		Floodplain		All respondents	
Adjusted for year	1998	2010	1998	2010	1998	2010
Consumer surplus (fitted demand)	591	791	1632	2184	1490	1994
Standard error	40	54	49	66	47	63
Observed SD	1239	1659	1942	2600	1915	2564
Consumer surplus (observed demand)	1165	1560	1448	1938	1415	1894
Standard error	24	32	30	40	29	39
Observed SD	1755	2350	2181	2920	2131	2853

Table 4.6 Estimates of the consumer surplus for flood insurance, low premium (dollars per policy)

	Non-required		Floodplain		All respondents	
Adjusted for year	1998	2010	1998	2010	1998	2010
Consumer surplus (fitted demand)	352	472	990	1326	866	1159
Standard error	23	30	29	39	26	35
Observed SD	696	932	1151	1540	1086	1454
Consumer surplus (observed demand)	638	854	852	1140	788	1054
Standard error	13	17	17	23	16	22
Observed SD	961	1286	1284	1718	1186	1588

The first potential source is that respondents on the floodplain have the highest risk relative to all other groups and should benefit more from purchasing insurance against flooding. The second potential source is that floodplain respondents are required to purchase insurance, in many cases, and this observed increased consumer surplus may be the effect of the regulatory requirement to purchase flood insurance. Using the available data, it is not possible to distinguish between the two sources, but the group of respondents not required to purchase flood insurance includes respondents sited on the floodplain. Accordingly, the consumer surplus for the voluntary purchase group is probably a more accurate depiction of the true consumer surplus for the NFIP.

If an insurance program is actuarially fair such that the claims and premiums are asymptotically equal, then this estimate can be compared to the associated values found by Farrow and Scott (2013). Farrow and Scott (2013) found an *ex ante* consumer surplus for the NFIP of up to 19 % of the expected losses using an expected utility estimating framework which is much smaller than the estimate found in this analysis.

There is a broad range between the results of the transformation using the fitted estimate of demand and the corresponding results of the transformation using the observed demand. Haab and McConnell (2002, 163) explain the difference is due to the concavity of the demand curve, which is normally convex toward the origin. Haab and McConnell note Tobit models should probably use the fitted estimate of demand due to the concavity, but also state the choice is a "subjective decision depending on the survey design and the confidence in data collection methods." Accordingly, both estimates are provided here.

4.5 Conclusion

Estimates are found for the consumer surplus of the NFIP. From a theoretical perspective, the estimates for the consumer surplus provide insight into how differently affected parties respond to market demands in the economic environment. The estimate controls for some risk factors, and importantly controls for the income of program participants. However, this estimate has some limitations. One limitation is the decision to exclude policyholders required to participate. Being required to participate relates to being located on a higher risk property, and higher risk should increase the consumer surplus for flood insurance. However, some significant proportion of required NFIP purchasers allow the coverage to lapse within a few years of initial purchase. Those lapses indicate those purchasers have no expected consumer surplus from the NFIP. Policyholders who are located in an increased risk zone but without a mortgage, therefore not triggering the NFIP requirement, could have a higher tolerance for risk or may, due to increased relative wealth, have a greater capacity to self-insurance against some risks.

Nevertheless, the analysis is the first attempt to find a consumer surplus for the NFIP using payment data. Prior studies cited in Chap. 2 note there is a decrease in wealth or housing prices associated with properties in higher risk zones. However, prior studies did not directly touch on the consumer surplus for flood insurance. The estimate also provides the first estimate of the consumer surplus for flood insurance could be the basis of an open market in flood insurance in the USA. The central results, based on voluntary actions of potential policyholders within 1000 feet of the coastline, indicate a substantial average consumer surplus per policy.

Chapter 5
Retrospective Analysis: Results

Using the data described in Chap. 3 and the consumer surplus for the National Flood Insurance Program (NFIP) estimated in Chap. 4, it is possible to conduct the benefit-cost analysis (BCA) of the NFIP and Flood Mitigation Assistance (FMA) programs. This estimation will use the model developed in Chap. 3 with the data to find the net social benefits (NSB). The results are subject to sensitivity analysis and interpretation.

5.1 Estimation Process and Discussion

The first step in the estimation is to aggregate the individual county-level records for premiums and claims into annual national figures for the insurance program. In addition, the state-level and county-level information for FMA grants is aggregated to the national level and broken down by year for the program. The summary table, following the initial aggregation, is available in Table 5.1.

The second preparatory step is to adjust each year's values to account for the social discount rate (SDR), creating a present value for year 2010. This step can be conducted prior to final values for each year provided it is performed consistently across all static values. Because the figures represent historical information, social discounting inflates a particular year's value by the cumulative SDR. As a result, prior spending increases in value as time passes. The results are presented in Table 5.2. The mean value, during the study period, of the SDR was 4.817 % with a range of values from 3.21 to 6.46 %. These figures are derived from the long-term borrowing rate for the US government by averaging monthly borrowing figures for the October–September period, to account for the US government's fiscal year.

At the end of this process, there is a dataset representing annualized amounts of the premiums, claims, coverage, and grants for the NFIP and FMA programs, with present value SDR adjusted to 2010 dollars. The dataset also includes the

J. Howard, II, *Socioeconomic Effects of the National Flood Insurance Program*, SpringerBriefs in Political Science, DOI 10.1007/978-3-319-29063-8_5

Table 5.1 NFIP premiums, claims, policies, grants, and expenses (nominal dollars)

Year	Premiums	Claims	Policies	Grants	Expenses
1996	1,275,142,562	827,788,942	3,693,018	928,908	20,562,000
1997	1,509,751,333	519,537,378	4,102,349	12,021,927	20,981,000
1998	1,668,235,535	886,210,419	4,235,117	14,906,886	21,610,000
1999	1,719,638,552	754,832,560	4,329,952	14,441,432	22,685,000
2000	1,723,812,790	251,720,536	4,369,074	17,166,934	24,333,000
2001	1,740,329,954	1,275,673,854	4,458,468	12,370,107	25,736,000
2002	1,802,277,733	432,350,618	4,519,798	10,660,750	28,798,000
2003	1,897,687,275	772,850,737	4,565,490	12,230,469	32,393,000
2004	2,040,786,564	2,220,079,025	4,667,376	18,933,819	32,663,000
2005	2,241,133,158	17,639,483,528	4,961,792	18,353,438	33,336,000
2006	2,604,712,840	638,772,642	5,514,675	23,077,677	36,496,000
2007	2,843,351,919	608,773,264	5,655,774	27,617,448	38,230,000
2008	3,066,725,391	3,415,230,017	5,684,268	105,828,960	45,642,000
2009	3,187,064,468	766,009,252	5,700,232	120,832,707	49,418,000
2010	3,353,755,725	758,008,836	5,646,726	72,689,815	52,149,000

Table 5.2 Socially discounted NFIP premiums, claims, grants, and expenses (2010 dollars)

Year	Premiums	Claims	Policies	Grants	Expenses
1996	2,426,968,104	1,575,523,725	7,028,890	1,767,983	39,135,482
1997	2,699,052,485	928,801,068	7,333,960	21,492,157	37,508,707
1998	2,824,937,152	1,500,680,620	7,171,613	25,242,848	36,593,689
1999	2,766,215,350	1,214,225,752	6,965,173	23,230,527	36,491,154
2000	2,611,746,264	381,381,419	6,619,578	26,009,597	36,866,893
2001	2,505,980,505	1,836,900,986	6,419,951	17,812,281	37,058,441
2002	2,476,360,054	594,057,054	6,210,279	14,648,051	39,568,939
2003	2,508,507,094	1,021,612,772	6,035,011	16,167,162	42,819,526
2004	2,586,304,130	2,813,522,812	5,915,001	23,994,971	41,394,065
2005	2,725,526,051	21,452,037,207	6,034,221	22,320,305	40,541,159
2006	3,023,783,544	741,544,394	6,401,928	26,790,631	42,367,820
2007	3,152,009,793	674,858,176	6,269,732	30,615,438	42,380,028
2008	3,271,590,627	3,643,376,269	6,063,992	112,898,610	48,691,004
2009	3,294,135,475	791,743,711	5,891,734	124,892,141	51,078,222
2010	3,353,755,725	758,008,836	5,646,726	72,689,815	52,149,000
Total	42,226,872,354	39,928,274,800	96,007,788	560,572,518	624,644,129

number of policies for each year, also SDR adjusted to 2010 count. With these basic adjustments completed, it is possible to find the annual NSB in 2010 dollars and aggregate the results to find the NSB of the NFIP over the study period.

5.1.1 Insurance Program

The insurance program's NSB will be calculated using Eq. (3.24),

$$\Delta S = \gamma\lambda - \varphi\mu - \zeta - m\zeta + m\kappa. \tag{5.1}$$

The annualized net social benefits are calculated by applying Eq. (5.1) for each year in the study period. This creates annualized NFIP NSB estimates for each year in 2010 dollars. The sources of the variables in the equation are:

- γ is the consumer surplus for flood insurance per policy,
- λ is the number of policies,
- φ is the administrative fee rate paid through the Write Your Own (WYO) program,
- μ is the amount of premiums paid to the NFIP,
- ζ is the cost of managing the NFIP to the government,
- m is the marginal excess tax burden (METB), and
- κ is the claims paid by the NFIP.

The annualized results are presented in Table 5.3. Therefore, the NSB due to the NFIP from 1996 to 2010 is computable by summing the annualized estimates of the NFIP's NSB. The sum is 78.38 billion dollars. The sum is the net social benefits notionally aggregated to 2010. Because the NFIP's benefits are presumed to occur contemporaneously with any transfer of benefit, there are no discounted future returns. Therefore, the year 2060 NSB of the NFIP are equal to the year 2010 NSB. The sensitivity of these results is investigated in Sect. 5.2.

Table 5.3 Socially discounted NSB for the NFIP (2010 dollars)

Year	NSB
1996	5,515,966,117
1997	5,554,072,291
1998	5,549,640,418
1999	5,324,271,950
2000	4,866,966,698
2001	5,089,640,477
2002	4,614,695,441
2003	4,573,754,248
2004	4,916,146,757
2005	9,648,860,463
2006	4,712,060,734
2007	4,570,301,012
2008	5,122,683,903
2009	4,266,941,714
2010	4,053,847,430
Total	78,379,849,652

5.1.2 Flood Mitigation Activities

Per the results of Rose et al. (2007), FMA grants have a point value estimate of benefit-cost ratio (BCR) of 5, based on the underlying assumption that the return period for an FMA grant is 50 years and an SDR of 2 %. Based on this information, it is possible to estimate an annualized rate of return for the average FMA project using a root-finding algorithm. When done, the annualized rate of return is approximately 15.91 %, for every year up to 50 years from the grant date. The value does not include any social discounting for future returns, therefore it is necessary to apply social discounting independently of the annualized rate of return.

This factor can be used with the previously socially discounted FMA grant amounts to find the net present value of each year's FMA grants over the study period. For the study period, the 15.91 % return for every year after the grant is made until 2010. The rate implies a payback period of approximately 6.3 years. The results of this process are given in Table 5.4.

The returns column of Table 5.4 shows a decreasing NSB in later years. This is due to the return rate for FMA projects having not yet returned the original investment, but artificially reduces the effects of later FMA grants to negative levels as the later grants have not been in place long enough to have earned a positive return. The point estimates of the NSB for the FMA program are created by summing the NSB for each year (Table 5.5).

Because of the bias against later projects, the cumulative NSB for the FMA projects is negative on a retrospective basis. Using the original estimate of the BCR for the FMA programs developed by Rose et al. (2007), the 50-year return on the FMA can be calculated. Using the BCR of 5, the NSB of the FMA through the year

Table 5.4 FMA grant returns by year (millions of 2010 dollars)

Year	Grants	Returns
1996	1,767,983	281,315
1997	21,492,157	3,683,984
1998	25,242,848	7,506,042
1999	23,230,527	10,826,659
2000	26,009,597	14,335,876
2001	17,812,281	16,458,998
2002	14,648,051	18,036,153
2003	16,167,162	19,924,175
2004	23,994,971	22,919,670
2005	22,320,305	25,545,762
2006	26,790,631	28,648,059
2007	30,615,438	32,227,956
2008	112,898,610	48,978,131
2009	124,892,141	67,325,898
2010	72,689,815	76,703,686

Table 5.5 Socially discounted NSB for the FMA (2010 dollars)

Year	NSB (2010)	NSB (forecast to 2060)
1996	−1,486,669	8,839,917
1997	−17,808,173	107,460,785
1998	−17,736,806	126,214,242
1999	−12,403,868	116,152,636
2000	−11,673,721	130,047,983
2001	−1,353,283	89,061,407
2002	3,388,102	73,240,255
2003	3,757,013	80,835,811
2004	−1,075,302	119,974,857
2005	3,225,457	111,601,523
2006	1,857,428	133,953,155
2007	1,612,518	153,077,191
2008	−63,920,479	564,493,049
2009	−57,566,243	624,460,706
2010	4,013,871	363,449,073
Total	−167,170,154	2,802,862,590

2060 can be calculated. This BCR assumes an SDR of 2 %. Based on these values, the NSB of the FMA program is −167.17 million dollars in 2010 with long-term NSB of 2.80 billion dollars to 2060.

It is useful to understand how the long-term returns to the FMA program provide additional gains in the NSB for the combined programs. While the analysis included here is a retrospective analysis, it is useful to estimate the long-term effects of past flood mitigation efforts to better understand the effects of the NFIP and FMA programs. In addition to capturing the long-term gains, such an analysis shows the 50- year difference in returns between the NSB to 2010 and the NSB to 2060. However, the 2060 figures are limited to not including grants or flood insurance activities following 2010 and only give the long-term NSB of the study period from 1996 to 2010. The values given for the long-term benefits to 2060 are given in the present value of 2010.

Following the creation of NSB estimates for both the NFIP and FMA programs, the last step necessary to create a point estimate is to add the two estimates. The NSB of the NFIP is estimated at 78.21 billion dollars in 2010 and long-term benefits to 2060 of 81.18 billion dollars. The NSB grows due to FMA returns increasing over time. The amounts paid through the insurance program to compensate claims are presumed to have no long-term returns. However, there is a long-term benefit from the FMA program, which doubles the NSB of the combined NFIP and FMA programs.

Of the inputs to the NFIP social surplus model and the FMA grants, the largest contributing factors are the change in the METB and the consumer surplus for the NFIP. As shown in Fig. 5.1, the METB for 2005 is roughly as large as the change in the consumer surplus. The large METB in 2005 is due to the assumption that

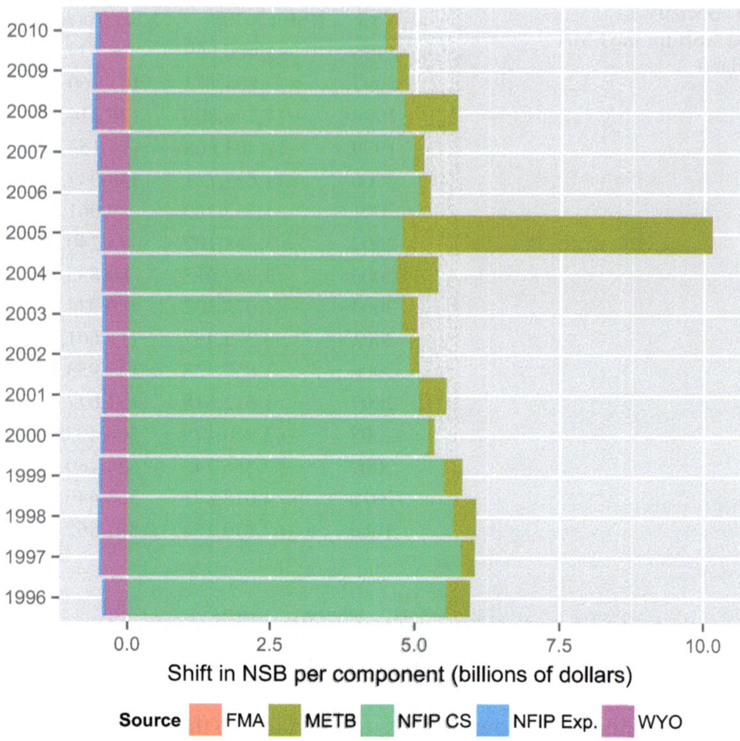

Fig. 5.1 Tornado plot of NSB per component by year

the NFIP's revenues offset the potential economic burden of taxes necessary to compensate flood victims through special payments if the NFIP did not exist. Since the amount of special payments is presumed to mirror the claims made against the NFIP, the amount of the METB varies accordingly. The METB is also positive in this analysis since the presumption is the taxes are not paid if the NFIP does exist.

The METB in 2005 is larger than other years due to the effects of two major hurricanes, Katrina and Rita, which struck the Gulf Coast causing major flooding. The effect of the METB on the results prompts the first two sensitivity tests. The first investigates the effect of the year 2005 on the results. The second investigates the effect of the METB on the results. The results of the base analysis and all of the sensitivity analyses are presented in Table 5.9.

The consumer surplus, however, is a consistently large benefit year-over-year that drives the analysis toward a positive NSB. The strength of the consumer surplus results, however, can be questioned due to the assumption that voluntary policyholders represent the average consumer, as presented in Chap. 4. Therefore, the consumer surplus's effects will also be analyzed in the sensitivity analysis.

5.2 Sensitivity Analysis

Sensitivity analysis can contribute to understanding these results by providing a measure of the uncertainty in the point estimates. There are two major approaches to the sensitivity analysis that will be used. The first involves excluding certain parameters from the sum, such as excluding a year or an element of the social surplus. The second is Monte Carlo simulation (MCS), which tests assumptions and results given uncertainty about some, but not all of the parameters of the analysis.

5.2.1 Effect of Hurricanes Katrina and Rita

In August 2005, Hurricane Katrina struck the Gulf Coast causing severe damage to Louisiana, Mississippi, and Texas. Katrina's most severe damage was to New Orleans, which was also hit by the large storm surge causing substantial flooding throughout the city. Katrina caused an estimated 1.2 million people to be evacuated from the Gulf Coast and 25.8 billion dollars in losses to the NFIP. In addition to the Gulf Coast damage, Katrina caused tornadoes and severe rainfall throughout the eastern USA. Katrina and related events killed more than 1800 people in the USA. Katrina is considered one of the worst natural disasters in American history (Knabb et al. 2005).

In September 2005, Hurricane Rita struck the Gulf Coast. While the damage was less severe, and concentrated along the Texas coastline, Rita was a large hurricane in its own right. Occurring only three weeks after Katrina, Rita extended the time required to remove flood waters from Katrina-affected areas. Rita and related events killed 55 people in the USA and, like Katrina, caused severe rainfall throughout the USA as the storm dissipated (Knabb et al. 2006).

To understand the effect of Hurricanes Katrina and Rita on the NSB of the NFIP, the simplest approach is to exclude the year 2005 from the dataset and perform the analysis. The year 2005 included a number of other smaller flood events. The data granularity does not permit elimination of transactions based on a particular event. Therefore, the simplest solution is to eliminate the year 2005 from the analysis. This includes the summary figure for the FMA program, despite the fact FMA grants from 2005 were not likely affected by the hurricanes.

Excluding 2005, the NSB of the NFIP is estimated at 68.56 billion dollars in 2010 and long-term benefits of 71.42 billion dollars. The positive NSB in 2010 shows there is a general benefit in current terms from the NFIP and FMA programs. In addition, the NSB of the results in 2060 are positive due to the long- term returns from the FMA program. These results suggest the benefits from the FMA program offset the costs of the NFIP program from a social accounting perspective, given an approximately average year of claims. Interpreted another way, the NSB of the NFIP and FMA programs increases with larger or more frequent flood disasters.

5.2.2 *Effect of the Marginal Excess Tax Burden*

The METB is justified on the grounds that a tax on any economic activity will affect the decision to engage in the activity at the margin (Office of Management and Budget 1992). If an individual chooses not to engage in an activity due to the increased cost caused by a tax, there is a greater economic loss caused by the tax. Therefore, BCA should include the potential loss in economic activity as a cost of a project.

In this analysis, the METB is a benefit because the METB is not lost in the case of the NFIP. The METB is only an economic loss if tax revenue is required to pay for flood recovery. Since the tax revenue is not required, the METB is a benefit. However, the assumption that the government would fund continued flood recovery is not necessarily valid and subject to investigation. To understand the effect of the METB on the results, it is useful to recalculate the results as if the ad hocpayments value in the social surplus is zero. This effectively excludes the METB benefits while still including the METB for the costs of operating the NFIP.

When excluding the METB from the social surplus estimate, the NSB of the NFIP is estimated at 68.23 billion dollars in 2010 and long-term benefits to 2060 of 71.20 billion dollars. While excluding the METB, this estimate does include the year 2005 non-METB costs and benefits. Both the current results and the long-term results from this sensitivity analysis are negative. Without the benefit of not tax-funding recovery efforts, the combined programs have a negative NSB. As the analytical assumption that the government would tax-fund relief programs in the absence of the NFIP is difficult to quantify, the negative results present a scenario in which the government performs no relief. In a sense, if viewing the NFIP as a standalone program with no associated political or historical environment, the NFIP has a negative NSB due to the large social costs of implementation. Further sensitivity analysis will examine the results with respect to a range of METB values and ad hocpayments.

5.2.3 *Effect of the Consumer Surplus*

As shown in Chap. 4, the consumer surplus is approximately 791 dollars per policy in 2010 dollars. This was based on a sample of potential policyholders who were not required to purchase flood insurance. Due to the sample, the result is likely biased and overstated due to the increased value a policyholder would receive from purchasing a flood insurance policy in a higher risk area. In addition, those who are required to purchase flood insurance would prefer not to have a consumer surplus of zero from the program, which would also reduce the average consumer surplus.

Accordingly, it is useful to understand the effect of the consumer surplus on the NSB estimates. This analysis includes a sensitivity analysis over the consumer surplus. Ideally, the analysis would find a break-even point for the percentage of policyholders being voluntary participants that would lead to a zero-dollar NSB for the NFIP. However, the NSB remains positive even if the consumer surplus from the NFIP's insurance program is zero. Excluding the consumer surplus, the NSB of the NFIP is estimated at 2.28 billion dollars in 2010 and long-term benefits to 2060 of 5.25 billion dollars.

There is an interaction between the regained ad hocpayments benefit and the consumer surplus for the NFIP that generates a large positive NSB. But both values are based on the broad assumptions of how potential policyholders behave in the marketplace. The interaction leads to the conclusion that if there were no voluntary flood insurance purchases and there was no expectation of a government-funded recovery effort, then the NSB of the NFIP would be negative.

5.2.4 *Monte Carlo Simulation: Simultaneous Uncertainty*

An MCS of the NFIP's costs and benefits is useful to understand the effect of the program and the relative effect of different features of the program on the NSB. As described in Sect. 3.2.1.8, some of the parameters are known to the limits of administrative accuracy while others are estimates. The MCS integrates assumptions about the statistical distribution for several variables. The distributional assumptions are for:

- The METB
- The consumer surplus for flood insurance
- The percentage paid to insurers in WYO fees, and
- The NSB of FMA programs

Each of these assumptions is based on estimated effect levels and is subject to sensitivity concerns. In contrast, other values such as the amount of claims paid into the NFIP or the value of grants given as part of the FMA are assumed to be known given the nature of this analysis. This is due to the retrospective orientation of the analysis. The variables included are the principal analytical variables and will show the distribution of the NSB beyond the base case. Beginning with Eq. (3.24),

$$\Delta S = \gamma\lambda - \varphi\mu - \zeta - m\zeta + m\kappa, \qquad (5.2)$$

four variables must be addressed in the sensitivity analysis.

Several variables are measured directly from historical data. The variables κ, μ, λ, and ζ are directly measured and are not estimates. While there can be some possible measurement error due to filing errors, the values of κ, μ, λ, and ζ that are derived directly from financial statements are considered to be accurate. The variables to be analyzed are listed in Table 5.6. The first variable to be investigated through the sensitivity analysis is γ, the amount of the consumer surplus from the NFIP per policy. The multiplier is estimated in Chap. 4 and a distribution for the multiplier is also estimated. The distribution is normal with mean 791 and standard deviation of 1659.

Table 5.6 Sensitivity analysis parameters

Variable	Distribution	Parameters
METB	Uniform	Lower bound: 0.18; Upper bound: 0.28
Fees paid to insurers	Uniform	Lower bound: 0.15; Upper bound: 0.17
Consumer surplus from the NFIP	Normal	Mean: 791; Standard deviation: 1659
FMA BCR	Log-normal	Mean: 5; Standard deviation: 1.1

The second variable to be analyzed is m, the METB. Based upon the work of Boardman et al. (2010), there is a range given for potential values from 0.18 to 0.28. The sensitivity of the METB on the results will be tested over the range of [0.18, 0.28] over a uniform distribution.

The third variable to be analyzed is φ, the WYO fees paid to producers. The value is fixed through the regulatory process with a lower bound of 0.15 and an upper bound of 0.17. The sensitivity analysis of value of the fees assumes a uniform distribution to model the expected value of the WYO fee percentage industry-wide.

The final variable to be analyzed as part of the sensitivity analysis is R, the BCR of the FMA program grants. The authors of the report note the distribution is log-normal and provide a standard deviation of 1.1, suitable for use in this sensitivity analysis.

The sensitivity analysis yields a mean NFIP NSB of the benefits to 2010 of 78.67 billion dollars (s.d. 160.33). There are 70.1 % positive trials from the MCS. Similarly, the analysis yields a mean NFIP NSB of the long-term benefits to 2060 of 81.65 billion dollars (s.d. 160.33). There are 70.6 % positive trials from the MCS. The distribution of the trials is shown in Fig. 5.2.

When excluding the effects of Hurricanes Katrina and Rita, the sensitivity analysis yields a mean NFIP NSB of the benefits to 2010 of 69.36 billion dollars (s.d. 150.24). There are 68.9 % positive trials from the MCS. Similarly, the analysis yields a mean NFIP NSB of the long-term benefits to 2060 of 72.23 billion dollars (s.d. 150.24). There are 69.5 % positive trials from the MCS. The distribution of the trials is shown in Fig. 5.3.

In the base case, the mean NSB of the sensitivity analysis is positive and the majority of trials tested had a positive NSB to 2010 and for long-term returns to 2060. Without the effects of Hurricanes Katrina and Rita, the mean NSB to 2010 and the long-term returns to 2060 were still positive as were the majority of MCS trials tested. However, the results were several billion dollars lower in each instance. With the NSB likely positive, under this uncertainty model, the base analysis showing a positive NSB is reinforced. Under these circumstances, it is useful to know how major variables respond to greater uncertainty. The first to be investigated is uncertainty in the ad hocpayments estimate.

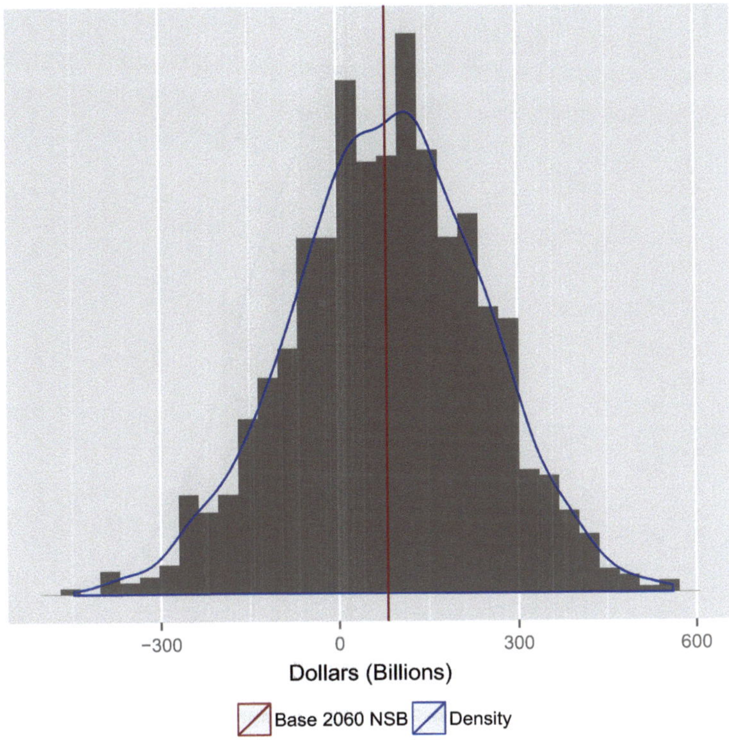

Fig. 5.2 Distribution of sensitivity analysis outcomes (year 2060)

5.2.5 Monte Carlo Simulation: Uncertainty in Ad Hoc Payments

This analysis relies on the assumption that there are gains in the NSB from the NFIP for not requiring taxpayers to fund direct grants and payments to flood disaster victims through ad hocpayments if the NFIP did not exist. The assumption is the ad hocpayments match the claims made in the event the NFIP does exist. However, the assumption has a large effect on the results as shown in Sect. 5.2.2. A special sensitivity analysis that uses stochastic simulation over the parameters of the ad hocpayments was used to test the effects of this assumption. This is accomplished by first estimating the distribution of claims at the national level per year. The distribution of the claim at the national level per year presumably follows a gamma distribution since the gamma distribution is frequently associated with modeling insurance claims (Embrechts et al. 1997).

Other options for simulating the distribution of claims include the generalized extreme value distribution and the Weibull distribution, both of which are also used to model claims or damages from extreme events. In general, all these models are

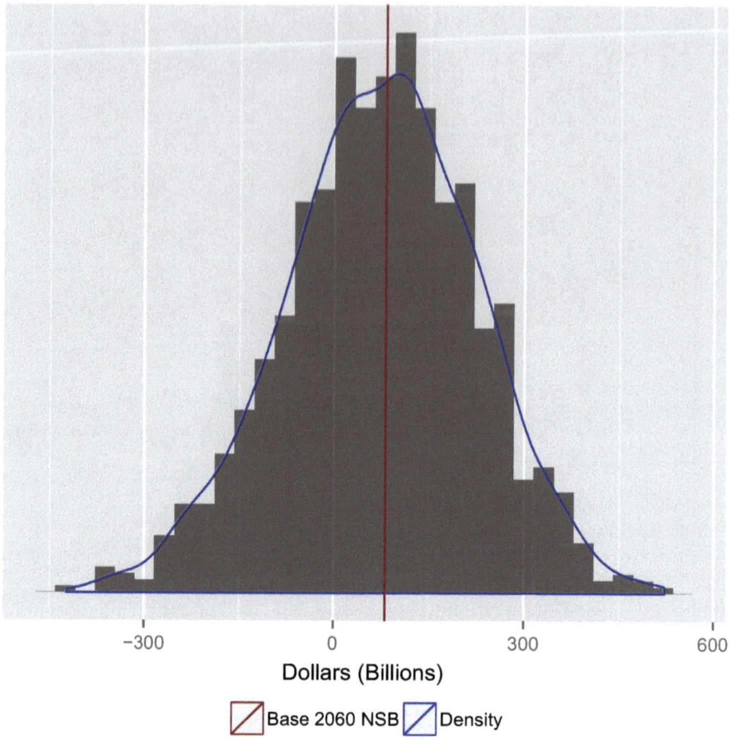

Fig. 5.3 Distribution of sensitivity analysis outcomes, excluding 2005 (year 2060)

Table 5.7 Sensitivity analysis parameters for ad hocpayments

Variable	Distribution	Parameters
Ad hocrecovery funds	Gamma	Shape: 0.788
		Scale: 2.69 billion

well suited to capture the extreme events frequently associated with weather-related modeling efforts. In this case, using 16 years of data, the gamma distribution is a good fit and simple to estimate. The parameters for the distribution are given in Table 5.7, which provide for a large scale. The scale of a gamma distribution describes the magnitude of the random variables generated. The shape of a gamma distribution describes the distribution's skewness. This estimation is based on the SDR-adjusted claims estimates, allowing them to include inflationary and other time-based adjustments necessary in a BCA.

For the purposes of this sensitivity analysis, all other variables input into this model are held static. Therefore, the only varying input is the amount of claims and the associated presumed effects of ad hocpayments made in the absence of the NFIP to property owners affected by flood disasters.

The sensitivity analysis yields a mean NFIP NSB to 2010 of 76.69 billion dollars (s.d. 8.57). There are 100 % positive trials from the MCS. Similarly, the analysis

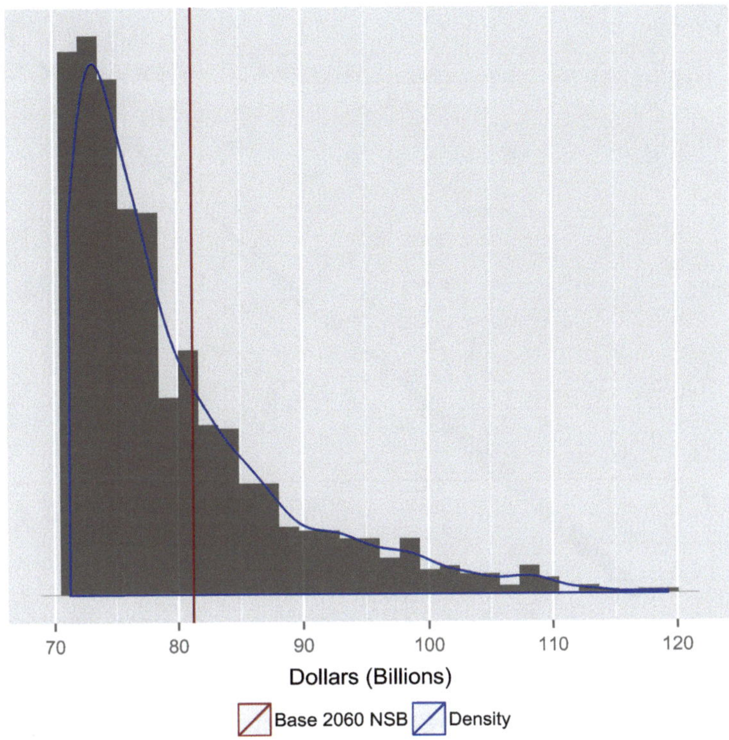

Fig. 5.4 Distribution of sensitivity analysis outcomes for ad hocpayments (year 2060)

yields a mean NFIP NSB of the long-term benefits to 2060 of 79.49 billion dollars (s.d. 8.57). There are 100 % positive trials from the MCS. Because the amount of claims is the key distinguishing feature between whether or not the effects of Hurricanes Katrina and Rita are included, the results for this sensitivity analysis without the year 2005 are not included. However, the effects of the hurricanes are included in the distribution of claims used in this sensitivity analysis (Figs. 5.4 and 5.5).

In this analysis, the mean NSB to 2010 are positive, and all of the simulated MCS trials tested are positive, as well. There is a long tail in the sensitivity analysis from the larger but less frequent flood events that are modeled through the gamma distribution. However, as the base NSB without ad hocpayments is positive, so are any possible NSB with ad hocpayments benefit added. This points to the importance of the amount of consumer surplus in finding the NSB under the social surplus model, which was also found through the special case analysis where the METB is zero.

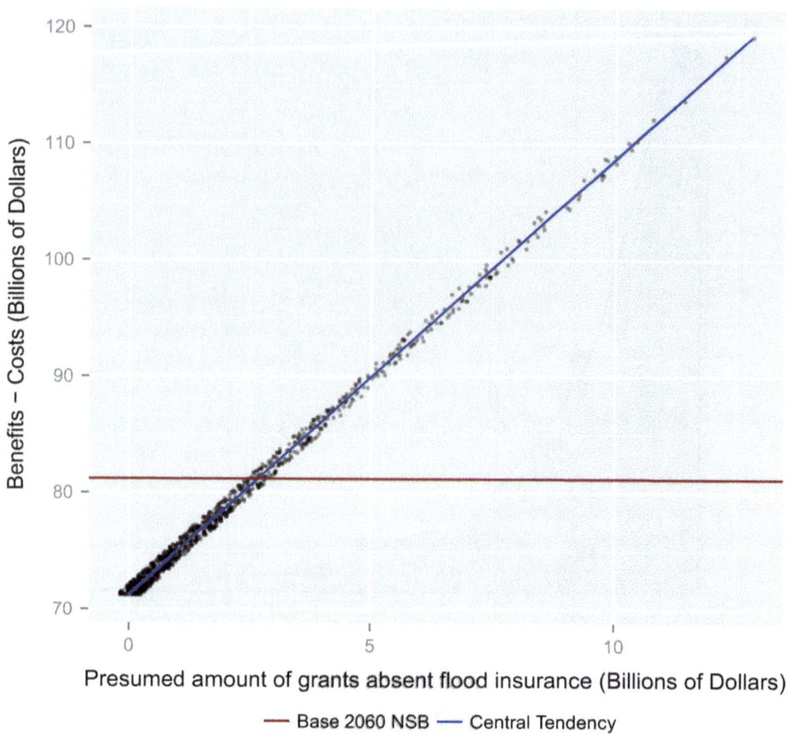

Fig. 5.5 Benefits–costs sensitivity to the expected claims for flood insurance (year 2060)

5.2.6 Monte Carlo Simulation: Uncertainty in Producer Surplus

This analysis integrates the assumption that the payments made to insurance companies to administer the NFIP are a pure economic cost to society. This assumption, if incorrect, may artificially reduce the gains to the NSB by failing to account for the benefits identified as producer surplus received by the insurance companies for administering the program. It is difficult to produce a reliable estimate for the gains attributable to the NFIP as insurance companies do not report profitability ratios on the administrative work.

This sensitivity analysis investigates the effects this assumption has on the NSB by varying two input variables to the model. The first variable is the amount of fees, which is varied between the upper and lower bounds as in the principal sensitivity analysis. Additionally, a new variable, ρ, representing a multiplier, models alternative assumptions about the producer surplus. The multiplier represents what portion of the fees are an economic cost in the producer surplus. In this sensitivity analysis, the variable ρ is varied with a lower bound of $0\,\%$. The lower bound is the case where the producer surplus is a total profit to the insurance companies. The upper

Table 5.8 Sensitivity analysis parameters for the producer surplus

Variable	Distribution	Parameters
Percent of fees as economic cost	Uniform	Lower bound: 0; Upper bound: 1
Fees paid to insurers	Uniform	Lower bound: 0.15; Upper bound: 0.17

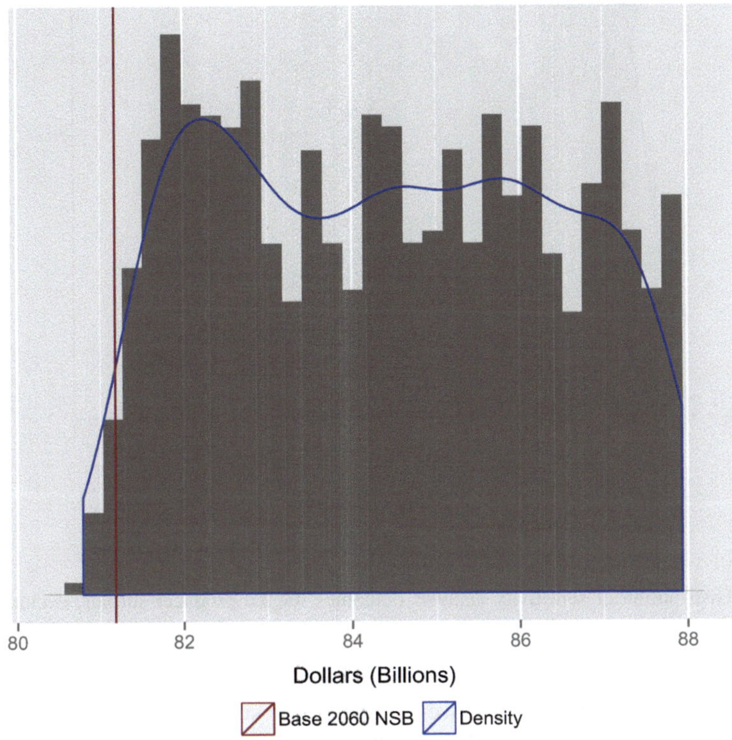

Fig. 5.6 Distribution of sensitivity analysis outcomes for the producer surplus (year 2060)

bound of variance is 100 %, where the insurance companies receive a total loss on the fees administering the program. For the purposes of this sensitivity analysis, all other variables input into this model are held constant (Table 5.8).

The sensitivity analysis yields a mean NFIP NSB to 2010 of 81.46 billion dollars (s.d. 1.98). There are 100 % positive trials from the MCS. Similarly, the analysis yields a mean NFIP NSB of the long-term benefits to 2060 of 84.43 billion dollars (s.d. 1.98). There are 100 % positive trials from the MCS. The distribution of trials for the analysis is shown in Fig. 5.6.

When excluding the effects of Hurricanes Katrina and Rita, the sensitivity analysis yields a mean NFIP NSB to 2010 of 72.30 billion dollars (s.d. 1.85). There are 100 % positive trials from the MCS. Similarly, the analysis yields a mean NFIP NSB of the long-term benefits to 2060 of 74.46 billion dollars (s.d. 1.85). There are 100.00 % positive trials from the MCS. The distribution of trials for the analysis is shown in Fig. 5.7.

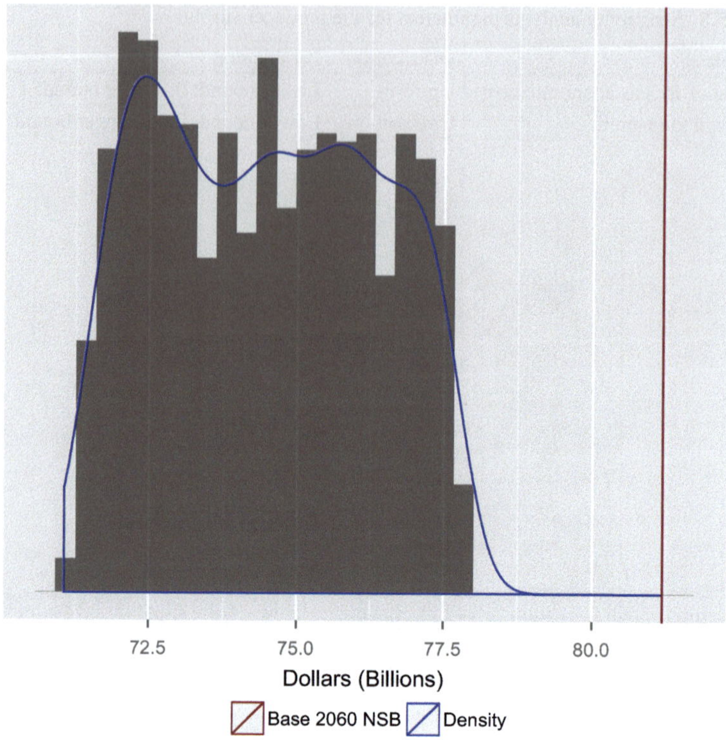

Fig. 5.7 Distribution of sensitivity analysis outcomes for the producer surplus, excluding 2005 (year 2060)

The sensitivity of the results over the producer surplus is interesting for being positive for all attempted trials. The result holds even in the case where the analysis excludes 2005. This is because the sensitivity analysis is conducted on the producer surplus, presumed negative in the base case, and reduces the effect from 100 % to 0 %. Accordingly, all of the results are incrementally larger than the base.

5.3 Conclusions

With the base case analysis and sensitivity analyses completed, it is possible to test the original hypothesis. The hypothesis asks if the NSB of the NFIP and FMA programs, combined, are greater than or equal to zero. If the results are positive, then the programs provide an NSB. If not, then the programs are a cost to the economy. The first hypothesis test is given by,

Table 5.9 Summary of BCA results (billions of dollars)

Value in year	2010	Forecast to 2060
Base analysis	78.21	81.18
Excluding 2005	68.56	71.42
Excluding METB	68.23	71.20
Excluding the NFIP consumer surplus	2.28	5.25
Sensitivity analysis mean	78.67	81.65
Sensitivity analysis mean (excluding 2005)	69.36	72.23
Sensitivity over ad hocpayments	76.69	79.49
Sensitivity over the producer surplus	81.46	84.43
Sensitivity over the producer surplus (excluding 2005)	72.30	74.46

H_0: The net present value of the social benefits of the NFIP from 1996 through 2010 were less than or equal to zero (0).

H_1: The net present value of the social benefits of the NFIP from 1996 through 2010 were greater than zero (0).

and the results of the base case estimate and the sensitivity analyses are given in Table 5.9.

The base case estimate for the net change in NSB caused by the NFIP and FMA programs is positive at 78.21 billion dollars in 2010 and 81.18 billion dollars forecast to 2060. In addition, when the effects of Hurricane Katrina are excluded from the analysis, the results remain positive with an NSB of 68.56 billion dollars in 2010 and 71.42 billion dollars forecast to 2060. Finally, when the sensitivity analysis is conducted, the results are positive for any potential change in the distribution of benefits or costs, with a minimum value of the change in NSB of −450.57 billion dollars and a maximum value of the change in NSB of 557.94 billion dollars.

Several variables contribute to the sensitivity of the NFIP program. An important variable in the sensitivity analysis is γ, the consumer surplus for flood insurance. It combines with the number of policies in force, λ. The coverage level, however, is fixed and known while the consumer surplus is estimated. So only the consumer surplus is varied for the sensitivity analysis and across a fairly small range. This variable is the crux of the analysis and the sensitivity to it is shown in Fig. 5.8. The consumer surplus is the most significant component of the NSB and shifts in the consumer surplus translate directly into changes in the NSB. In addition, the sensitivity analysis presumes a normal distribution for the consumer surplus. The large number of zeros estimated when calculating per policy consumer surplus values leads to a large standard deviation. This is because, empirically, there is a large spread in the amount of flood insurance purchased by potential policyholders. Accordingly, there is a broad range for potential consumer surplus values estimated and an MCS over the consumer surplus is over a broad range. Figure 5.8 shows how very large, very small, and negative consumer surplus values affect the NSB. Lower consumer surplus values lead to lower estimates of the NSB for the NFIP and negative NSB are possible with a sufficiently large and negative consumer surplus estimate.

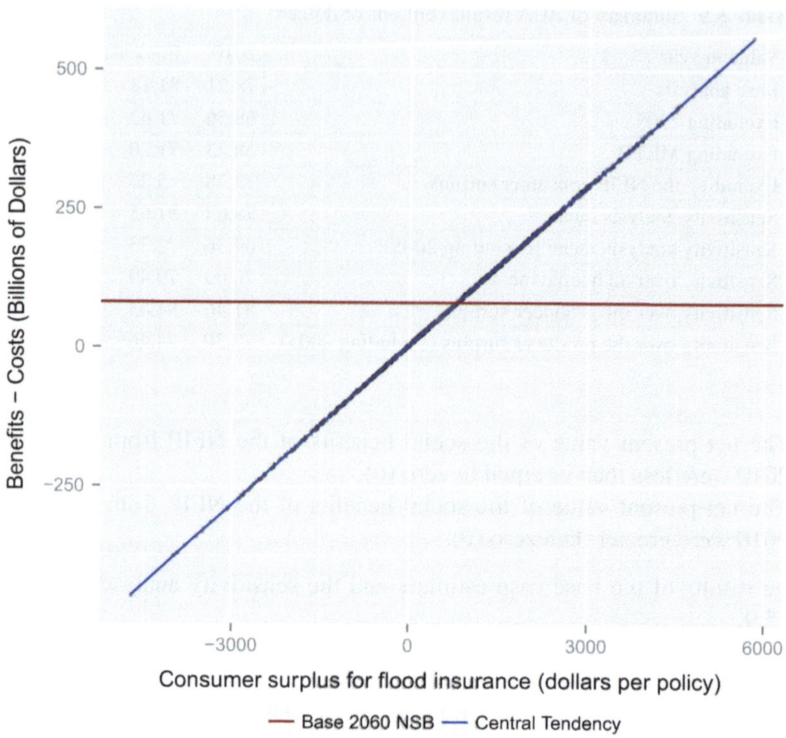

Fig. 5.8 Benefits–costs sensitivity to the consumer surplus for flood insurance (year 2060)

The second contributor to the sensitivity analysis is the METB, represented by *m*. This value is constrained by the specifications of the Office of Management and Budget (OMB), and so there is little shift due to this. However, when the ad hocpayments were tested over the range from zero through the amount of claims, the results remained positive, as shown in Fig. 5.9. This is also true of the potential variance in the WYO fees paid to insurers. Finally, though the FMA grants have a net social benefit of five times their value, the amount of grants is small compared to the NFIP finances. The FMA grants, however, push the NSB positive after accounting for the long-term returns in several of the analyses.

These results and sensitivity analyses indicate the US society is better off during this period with the NFIP than without. Numerous assumptions including the default BCA standard of omitting distributional effects are tested. However, several of the design decisions made in this analysis should be addressed. One such design decision focused on which estimate to use for the consumer surplus. Two different models presuming two different premium payment levels were developed. However, the BCA only used the higher value for premiums, which is associated with a lower deductible for policyholders. This decision is based on reports of its common use. Overall, the decision increases the NSB to society by approximately 319.38 dollars

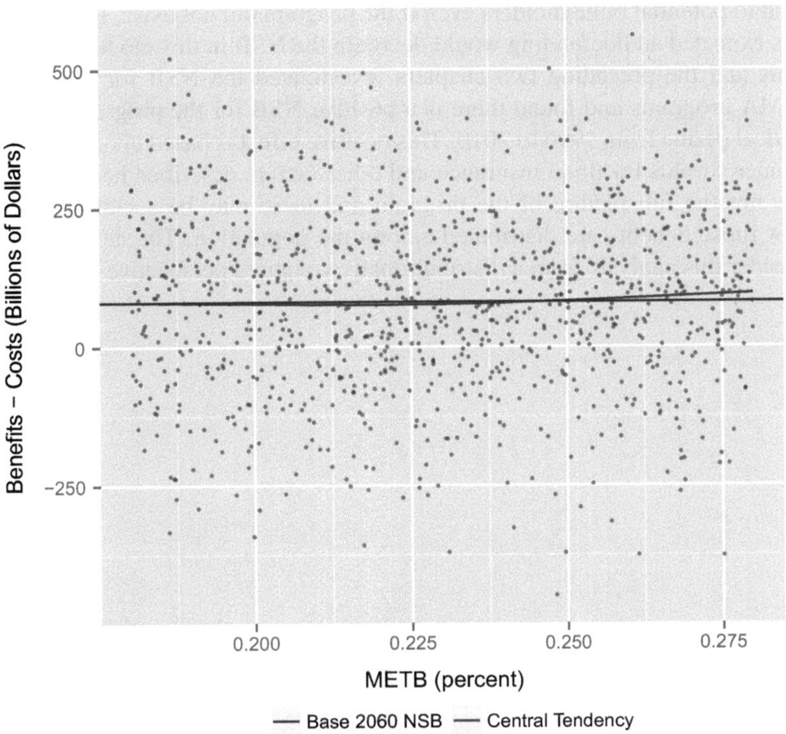

Fig. 5.9 Benefits–costs sensitivity to flood insurance METB (year 2060)

per policy, in 2000 dollars. Comparatively, the NSB of the programs would decrease by 30.7 billion dollars when the high-premium estimate for the NFIP's consumer surplus is used.

Another design decision focused on the treatment of the WYO fees paid to insurers. This analysis assumes those fees paid for the costs of implementing the program by producers and are simply subtracted from the NSB as such. However, it may be reasonable to consider this as a profit-making activity by producers, some percentage of the WYO fees would be added to the NSB. One possibility would be to use the industry average profitability to calculate such a percentage, but this can cause some analytical difficulty. For instance, industry profitability is not generally constant and involves unrelated business activities. This can also cause analytical problems if a major industry event, such as a severe hurricane, caused non-flood losses to the industry, it would lower the positive effect for that year, despite the clear benefits to the industry provided by the NFIP providing flood coverage. Because of the reversed effects, this analytical approach is not used.

The remaining major design decision, the presumption that if the government did not provide flood insurance, it would pay for flood recovery through other means, is important in the results. This is apparent in the final model, which expects funds to be paid to potential policyholders even if the program did not exist. The elimination of this expected ad hocfunding would decrease the NSB in this model.

This and the preceding two chapters investigated the NSB for the NFIP and the FMA programs and found there is a positive NSB for the programs during the analytical period from 1996 to 2010. This positive effect is based upon the estimated consumer surplus for flood insurance and other factors described herein. However, this is not the full picture of the program and there may be social good created in how those benefits are distributed among the population. The next chapter will reconsider this analysis from a distributionally weighted perspective.

Chapter 6
Distributionally Weighted Analysis

Distributional analysis provides a challenge to benefit-cost analysis (BCA). Standard BCA treats all parties equally and a distributional analysis alters that premise. Distributional analysis studies the ways in which distribution of funds affects different social classes based on economic or social status. With respect to BCA, distributional analysis can change the way standing is measured and reweight the effects for different social groups. Therefore, one approach to distributional analysis in BCA is to alter who has standing. For instance, Chap. 7 presents a BCA of the National Flood Insurance Program (NFIP) where the only party with standing is the federal government. Other standing restrictions can be created for different analyses.

Other approaches use more nuanced weighting schemes to provide insight. Ideally, an analysis of each policyholder complete with income and asset information would provide the best analysis of the distributional effects of the NFIP. However, the Federal Emergency Management Agency (FEMA) does not make policyholder level data available. Information is provided at the county level for both the flood insurance and Flood Mitigation Assistance (FMA) components of the NFIP. Given the differences in income and inequality between different counties, this a reasonable level ofanalysis. Weighting schemes may be based on income or asset holdings of particular classes of individuals. Using county-level information combined with known relative differences in median income from county to county, it is possible to weight each county with respect to each other. The weighting scheme used is based on the Atkinson index of income inequality (Atkinson 1970). This increases the marginal effect of NFIP funds in counties with lower income levels and decreases the marginal effect in counties with higher income levels.

J. Howard, II, *Socioeconomic Effects of the National Flood Insurance Program*, SpringerBriefs in Political Science, DOI 10.1007/978-3-319-29063-8_6

6.1 Methodology

The distributional analysis of the NFIP will be completed using the county-level data provided by FEMA for the finances of the program. However, the FMA grants are not necessarily given at the county level. Some grants are awarded to cities and some are awarded to counties. Aggregating city-level grants to their respective counties is possible. However, some grants are awarded to state agencies, such as a state natural resources department, for statewide effect. Other FMA grants are categorized by FEMA for statewide applicability.

These are more difficult to allocate to counties within their respective states because the allocation scheme would introduce a bias into any distributional analysis. For instance, allocating a statewide grant by population would increase the equity in the final analysis. Alternatively, distributing them by population would decrease the equity in the final analysis. This analysis adopts a middle of the road approach and assigns the median weight, 1, to all grants for which the finer-grained distributional effects cannot be ascertained.

The amounts of payments vary widely from county to county, under both the insurance and FMA components. In addition, each county has different income levels and different degrees of income inequality driven by each county's unique economic patterns. As a result, the NFIP insurance payments and FMA grants have a different economic effect in each county. The net social benefits (NSB) with distributional analysis is the sum of the county-level NSB with distributional analysis for both the insurance and FMA programs.

The basic sufficient statistic for the NFIP is identical under a weighted analysis. Additionally, the FMA grants are studied using the same method. However, before the annualized aggregates are collected, the individual county-level figures, for both NFIP finances and FMA grant allocations, are adjusted by a distributional weighting factor that increases or decreases the effect of a particular county's relationship with the NFIP in relation to the county's mean income. Counties with lower mean income receive a more favorable effect from the programs. To accomplish this weighting, the counties are rank-ordered based on income and weights are established for each county based on rank and relative income. Each county's average income will serve as a proxy for personal income.

The counties shall be grouped by quintiles and weights selected from Table 6.1. The weights themselves stem from the treatment of the marginal utility of income. Farrow (2011) explains BCA normally treats the marginal utility as constant across all groups. Therefore, $U(y_i) = cy_i$ for some constant c where $U(y_i)$ is the utility function and y_i is the ith group. For some aversion to income inequality, ϵ, then $U(y, \epsilon) = cy^{-\epsilon}$. Therefore,

$$\frac{U(y,\epsilon)}{U(\bar{y},\epsilon)} = \left(\frac{cy_i^{-\epsilon}}{c\bar{y}^{-\epsilon}}\right) = \left(\frac{y_i^{-\epsilon}}{\bar{y}^{-\epsilon}}\right) = \left(\frac{y_i}{\bar{y}}\right)^{-\epsilon} = \left(\frac{\bar{y}}{y_i}\right)^{\epsilon}. \tag{6.1}$$

Table 6.1 Atkinson distributional weights (Farrow 2011)

	Atkinson distributional weight				
Quintile	$\epsilon = 0.0$	$\epsilon = 0.25$	$\epsilon = 0.50$	$\epsilon = 0.75$	$\epsilon = 1.0$
First (0–20 %)	1.0	1.4	2.1	3.0	4.3
Second (20–40 %)	1.0	1.1	1.3	1.5	1.7
Third (40–60 %)	1.0	1.0	1.0	1.0	1.0
Fourth (60–80 %)	1.0	0.9	0.8	0.7	0.6
Fifth (80–100 %)	1.0	0.7	0.5	0.4	0.3

Accordingly, the weighting is equal to the mean income divided by the group income, taken to the power of the income aversion factor. In the case where $\epsilon = 0$, the relative weightings for each group are 1 and is the same as the normal BCA treatment. In this analysis, the case where $\epsilon = 0$ is identical to the analysis in Chap. 5. Farrow (2011) provides quintile weights for the USA when $\epsilon = \{0.0, 0.25, 0.5, 0.75, 1.0\}$.

In addition, counties will be reordered for each year of analysis to allow for relative changes in income that may shift relative weights. Following the initial weighting of each county's NFIP figures, the analysis will follow the same procedures as described in Chaps. 3 and 5.

6.2 Estimation Process

The first step in the estimation process is to distributionally weight each county's observations based on the relative incomes of each county. This begins with the NFIP financial data, as described in Appendix B, which is merged with the FMA grant information to which is also described at the county level. However, in slightly more than one-quarter of the grants provided under the FMA, the county receiving the grant cannot be resolved due to the grant being made to a state agency. In these cases, a new entry in the merged dataset is created that has no county descriptor. The end result of this is a dataset that contains the financial and grant data broken down by county and year, though county may be null.

Following this assembly, the dataset is merged with another dataset, called the weightset, that provides the relative weights at each of the five distributional weighting levels. The weightset is at the county level for every year of the study period. However, as the United States Census Bureau (USCB) does not provide county-level income data for 1996, the county-level income data for 1997 is used for that year. The weights were assigned to each county by sorting the counties by median income and assigning the appropriate weightset to each quintile.

After the weightset data has merged with the financial data, some elements may be missing weightsets. This includes those entries in the financial dataset for which there is no county, such as state grants. This also includes Kalawao County, Hawaii, for which income information was not available over several years in the study period. In these instances, the most conservative option is to weight NFIP financial transfers with a weight of 1. This is equivalent to not weighting the entries at all but is also the median for each weightset. While it may be possible to allocate statewide grants to the local level using different methods, such as those based on population, income, or implied risk, the simple method of median selection introduces no systemic bias as other potential methods might.

The county-level datasets are then copied once for each of the five Atkinson-weighting levels described in the Sect. 6.1. Then for each of the new panel datasets, the values of premiums, policies, and grants are then multiplied by the Atkinson weight for the county of interest. This yields five county-level panel datasets representing the local effects of the NFIP and FMA programs at different distributional weighting levels.

Following distributional weighting, the county-level information is aggregated by year, to give a single annualized national figure for premiums, claims, policies, and grants for the NFIP and FMA. Since the aggregation does not span multiple years, there is no need to include any adjustment for inflation. This process is repeated for each of the Atkinson-weighted panel datasets. An example summary table for the programs by year with Atkinson weights for $\epsilon = 0.5$ is available in Table 6.2.

The last step is to adjust each year's values to account for the social discount rate (SDR), to compute the present value. This step can be conducted prior to final values for each year provided it is performed consistently across all static values. Because the figures represent historical information, social discounting inflates a

Table 6.2 Atkinson-weighted ($\epsilon = 0.5$) NFIP premiums, claims, policies, and grants (nominal dollars)

Year	Premiums	Claims	Policies	Grants
1996	1,049,518,722.8	718,835,745.8	3,693,018.0	947,134.1
1997	1,241,895,905.0	438,919,767.6	4,102,349.0	9,699,461.2
1998	1,349,736,463.8	784,953,761.1	4,235,117.0	13,126,107.8
1999	1,349,905,041.0	645,846,649.4	4,329,952.0	12,305,573.7
2000	1,346,581,445.4	231,688,144.4	4,369,074.0	14,389,797.4
2001	1,386,350,991.6	759,463,252.0	4,458,468.0	10,634,545.1
2002	1,450,160,777.3	393,561,315.0	4,519,798.0	9,576,561.4
2003	1,583,706,609.3	600,597,282.5	4,565,490.0	10,160,435.2
2004	1,685,987,380.6	1,789,609,484.7	4,667,376.0	17,021,751.2
2005	1,739,882,169.3	23,376,942,570.1	4,961,792.0	16,254,347.1
2006	1,902,847,347.2	467,209,082.8	5,514,675.0	17,919,540.1
2007	2,081,132,665.3	427,685,359.3	5,655,774.0	18,575,013.8
2008	2,318,036,613.6	2,276,783,365.4	5,684,268.0	75,072,562.8
2009	2,523,668,677.0	585,803,439.2	5,700,232.0	93,589,286.3
2010	2,634,850,330.1	599,404,134.1	5,646,726.0	57,420,620.1

Table 6.3 Atkinson-weighted ($\epsilon = 0.5$) socially discounted NFIP premiums, claims, and grants (2010 dollars)

Year	Premiums	Claims	Grants
1996	1,997,540,150	1,368,154,024	1,802,672
1997	2,220,194,912	784,677,227	17,340,177
1998	2,285,600,925	1,329,215,807	22,227,335
1999	2,171,460,998	1,038,910,714	19,794,780
2000	2,040,203,600	351,030,372	21,801,961
2001	1,996,270,046	1,093,585,788	15,313,167
2002	1,992,545,408	540,759,896	13,158,357
2003	2,093,463,616	793,915,080	13,430,835
2004	2,136,664,462	2,267,985,532	21,571,793
2005	2,115,935,933	28,429,576,240	19,767,521
2006	2,208,995,328	542,378,075	20,802,604
2007	2,307,048,416	474,112,414	20,591,410
2008	2,472,887,491	2,428,878,419	80,087,605
2009	2,608,452,575	605,483,796	96,733,465
2010	2,634,850,330	599,404,134	57,420,620

particular year's value by the cumulative SDR since that year. As a result, prior spending increases in value as time goes on. This process is repeated for each of the Atkinson-weighted panel datasets. A sample estimate of the socially discounted annualized figures with Atkinson weights for $\epsilon = 0.5$ is in Table 6.3.

Three components of the social surplus model for the NFIP are handled in special ways. The first component is the number of policies in force, λ. While not a dollar figure, the number of policies in force is multiplied by a dollar figure, the consumer surplus. Since the policies in force are available at the county level, it is subject to SDR-adjustment, like in Chap. 5. The policies-in-force component is also subject to Atkinson weighting for the same reason. In both cases, the results are mathematically equivalent to weighting the consumer surplus estimate for each county or socially discounting the consumer surplus. The second and third components are ζ, the amount of NFIP expenses, and κ, the amount of claims paid out. This variable ζ is a national figure and is not Atkinson-weighted. The variable κ is used for assessing a tax effect, not actual payments, and is not Atkinson-weighted.

At the end of this process, there are five panel datasets representing annualized estimates of the premiums, claims, coverage, policies, and grants for the NFIP and FMA programs (Table 6.4). These panel datasets are distributionally weighted using the Atkinson weights as described in socially discounted 2010 dollars. With these basic adjustments completed, it is possible to aggregate the panel datasets to find the NSB of the NFIP for each alternative Atkinson-weight level.

The insurance program's NSB will be calculated using an Atkinson-weighted form of Eq. (3.24),

$$\Delta S = \gamma\lambda' - \varphi\mu' - \zeta - m\zeta + m\kappa, \tag{6.2}$$

Table 6.4 Atkinson-weighted ($\epsilon = 0.5$) socially discounted FMA grants (2010 dollars)

Year	Grants	Returns	NSB
1996	1,802,672.3	281,314.5	−1,521,357.7
1997	17,340,176.8	3,683,983.6	−13,656,193.2
1998	22,227,334.7	7,506,042.3	−14,721,292.4
1999	19,794,780.0	10,826,659.5	−8,968,120.5
2000	21,801,961.2	14,335,875.9	−7,466,085.3
2001	15,313,166.7	16,458,998.1	1,145,831.4
2002	13,158,357.1	18,036,153.5	4,877,796.4
2003	13,430,834.5	19,924,175.2	6,493,340.7
2004	21,571,793.0	22,919,669.7	1,347,876.7
2005	19,767,520.9	25,545,761.9	5,778,241.0
2006	20,802,604.3	28,648,059.2	7,845,454.9
2007	20,591,410.1	32,227,955.9	11,636,545.8
2008	80,087,605.3	48,978,130.8	−31,109,474.5
2009	96,733,464.7	67,325,898.4	−29,407,566.3
2010	57,420,620.1	76,703,685.6	19,283,065.4

where λ' is the Atkinson-weighted number of policies in force and μ' is the Atkinson-weighted amount of premiums paid to the NFIP by policyholders. The variables γ, φ, ζ, and κ have the same meaning as in Eq. (3.24). The variable κ is not Atkinson-weighted since its purpose in Eq. (6.2) is to represent the amount of money that would be raised nationally via taxation if the NFIP did not exist. Accordingly, it would be inappropriate to apply a weighting method to κ.

For each panel dataset representing the Atkinson-weighted and socially discounted values, annualized net social benefits are calculated by applying Eq. (6.2) for each year in the study period. This creates annualized NFIP NSB estimates for each year for every Atkinson-weight level. The sources of the variables in Eq. (6.2) are:

- γ is the *ex ante* willingness to pay for flood insurance per policy,
- λ' is the Atkinson-weighted number of policies,
- φ is the percentage of the fees paid to producers through the Write Your Own (WYO) program
- μ' is the Atkinson-weighted amount of premiums paid to the NFIP,
- m is the marginal excess tax burden (METB), and
- κ is the non-weighted accumulated claims paid by the NFIP.

Therefore, the NSB due to the insurance component of the NFIP from 1996 through 2010 at different Atkinson-weight levels is computable by summing the annualized estimates of the NFIP's NSB for each of the panel datasets. The Atkinson-weighted FMA annual totals are created in the same manner.

After the creation of Atkinson-weighted annual NSB values for the NFIP and FMA programs, the Atkinson-weighted NSB for the programs can be calculated using the same method as in Sects. 5.1.1 and 5.1.2. In addition to replicating the base analysis for each Atkinson-weighted case, this analysis will replicate the sensitivity

Table 6.5 NSB by Atkinson distributional weight (billions of dollars)

	Atkinson distributional weight				
	$\epsilon = 0.0$	$\epsilon = 0.25$	$\epsilon = 0.50$	$\epsilon = 0.75$	$\epsilon = 1.0$
	Base case analysis				
NFIP NSB	78.21	69.21	64.28	62.69	62.20
NFIP NSB (year 2060)	81.18	71.74	66.54	64.84	64.27
	Excluding 2005				
NFIP NSB	68.56	60.18	55.59	54.13	53.67
NFIP NSB (year 2060)	71.42	62.60	57.76	56.18	55.66
	MCS, simultaneous uncertainty				
Mean NFIP NSB	79.88	62.97	64.52	63.48	71.56
Std. dev. NFIP NSB	158.69	140.01	128.93	125.30	119.62
Percent greater than 0	69.60	66.40	69.00	69.50	71.90
	MCS, simultaneous uncertainty (forecast to 2060)				
Mean NFIP NSB	82.87	65.51	66.78	65.63	73.65
Std. dev. NFIP NSB	158.68	140.01	128.93	125.30	119.62
Percent greater than 0	70.60	67.10	69.90	70.10	72.50

analysis for excluding the effects of Hurricanes Katrina and Rita, as in Sect. 5.2.1, and add the Monte Carlo simulation (MCS) over simultaneous uncertainty, as in Sect. 5.2.4. Replicating these sensitivity analysis components will show how changing the distributional weightings also effects the limited analysis. The results of the base case analysis and sensitivity analyses are included in Table 6.5.

6.3 Results and Conclusions

Distributional weighting is a special case of sensitivity analysis. However, this analysis has separated the distributional weighting into a secondary analysis to provide a clearer view into the effects of Atkinson weighting on an analysis of the NFIP. Like for the unweighted analysis in Chap. 5, the distributionally weighted NSB is also positive across several different weightsets but decreasing as the aversion to income inequality is increased. Because the model for the NSB is otherwise identical, the distributionally weighted results are driven by the same factors as the purely retrospective results and reflect the same design decisions in similar ways. From that perspective, distributional weighting is insufficient to shift the nature of the results.

The first hypothesis test is given by,

H_0: The net present value of the distributionally weighted social benefits of the NFIP from 1996 through 2010 were less than or equal to zero (0).

H_1: The net present value of the distributionally weighted social benefits of the NFIP from 1996 through 2010 were greater than zero (0).

For all distributional weighting levels, the NSB for the NFIP and FMA programs is positive. In addition, when the effects of Hurricane Katrina are excluded from the analysis, the results remain positive. Finally, when the sensitivity analysis is conducted, the results are positive for any potential change in the distribution of benefits or costs.

However, distributional weighting, in this analysis, effects those summary estimates that are disaggregated at the local jurisdictional level. So the number of policies, represented by λ, is adjusted for local income levels. This is also true of the WYO payments to insurers, which presumes a local level, and therefore weightable aspect to its value from BCA perspective. However, the METB, which is a function of the claims level in this analysis, is not distributionally weighted since it is calculated at the national level based on a national-level understanding of the effect on the broader economy from taxation. Like the baseline estimate, the MCS is similarly affected by the distributional weighting. At no distributional weighting does a Monte Carlo outcome ever drop below zero NSB. This stems from the same analytical processes that affected the analysis in Chap. 5. Figures 6.1 and 6.2 show the distribution of MCS results from this analysis in both the base case and without the year 2005 included.

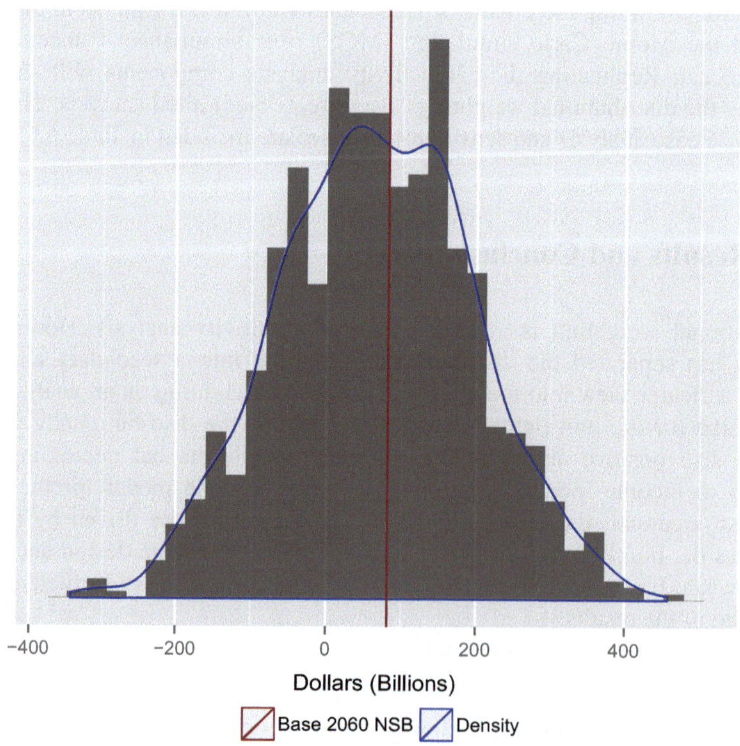

Fig. 6.1 Histogram of sensitivity analysis outcomes for $\epsilon = 0.5$ (forecast to year 2060)

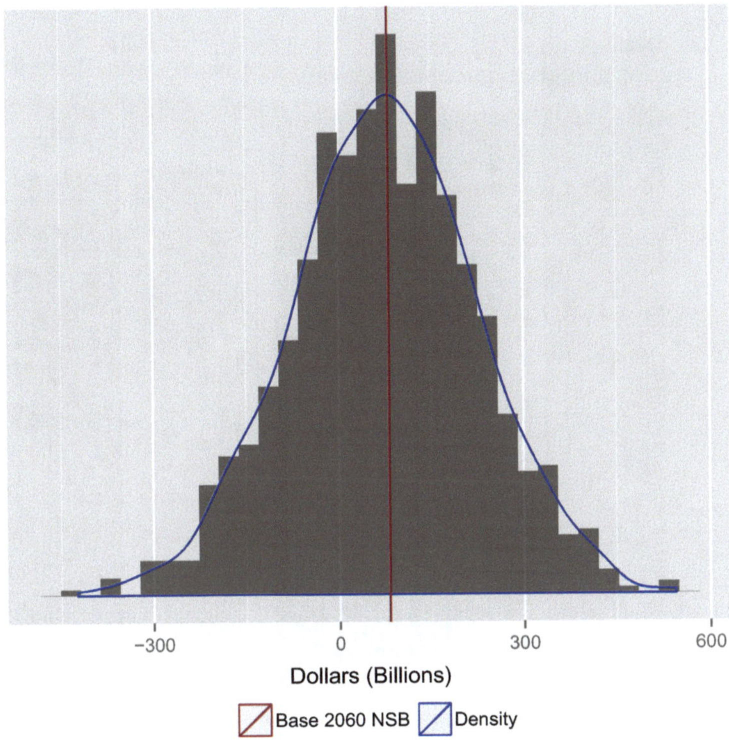

Fig. 6.2 Histogram of sensitivity analysis outcomes for $\epsilon = 0.5$, excluding 2005 (forecast to year 2060)

Despite these consistent outcomes for the NSB, there is another important result from this analysis. Figure 6.3 shows how the distributionally weighted NSB for the NFIP and FMA programs changes at different ϵ-levels for distributional weighting. This figure shows that the NSB decreases as the income aversion factor increases. This reflects the underlying consumer surplus structure in which claims tend to be more for those living in local jurisdictions with higher incomes in general. This does not demonstrate that policies are principally held by wealthier individuals but it does suggest a regressive redistributional effect to the NFIP, in the sense that a larger proportion of the benefits go to wealthier counties than costs from those counties.

This disagrees with prior research by Bin et al. (2011) who found a slightly progressive redistributional effect to the NFIP, based on the distribution of NFIP claims and premiums. Figure 6.4 shows the distributionally weighted NSB for the NFIP and FMA programs if the year 2005 effects, which include the effects of Hurricanes Katrina and Rita, are removed. Except for the starting point, these two graphs are very similar and reveal a somewhat consistent effect of the program.

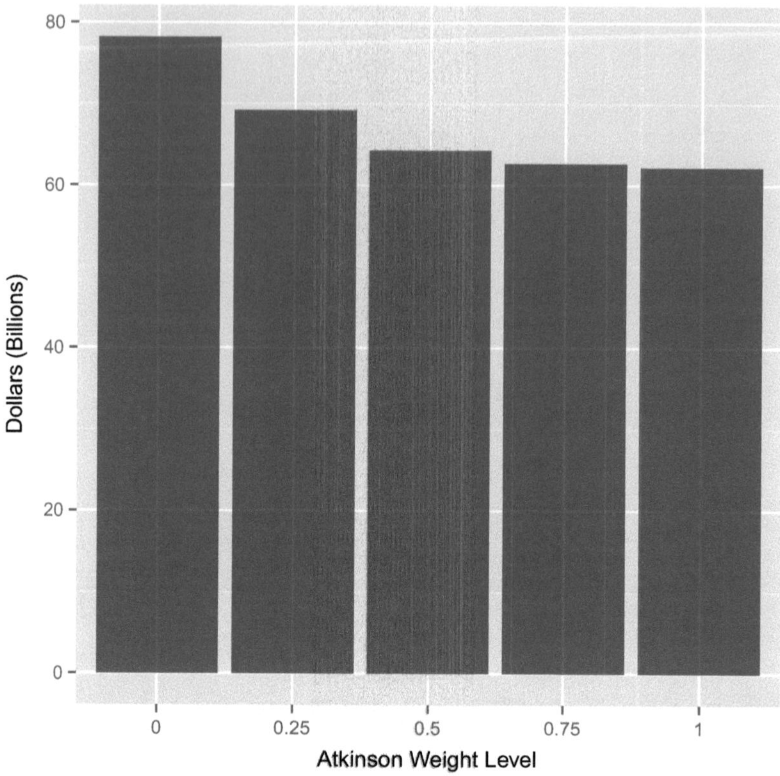

Fig. 6.3 Plot of NSB by ϵ-level

This chapter has further investigated the NSB of the NFIP and FMA programs by adding several distributional weighting methods. The main results are unchanged, though the distributional pattern of benefits varies depending on the proposed aversion to income inequality. The next chapter will further investigate the NFIP by evaluating the effects on government revenues and outlays.

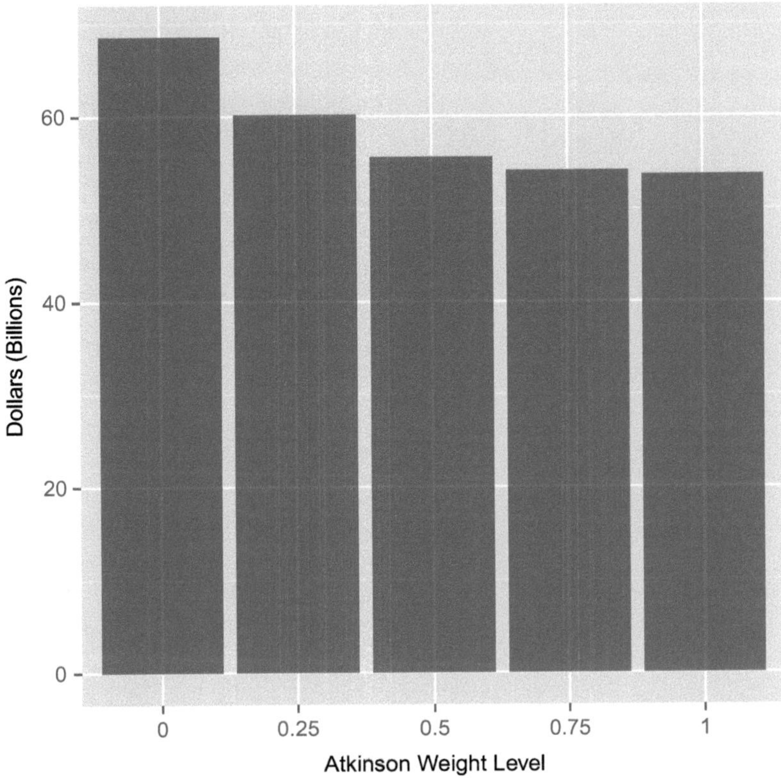

Fig. 6.4 Plot of NSB by ϵ-level, excluding 2005

Chapter 7
Governmental Income Analysis

The effect on government revenue stems from the question of whether or not the National Flood Insurance Program (NFIP) has reduced the cost to the government of flood events. This was, per Chaps. 1 and 2, a key reason for creating the NFIP. This analysis will refer to the time period from 1996 through 2010, like the other retrospective analyses included in this evaluation.

Unlike the other analyses, standing is restricted to just the federal government. This might seem unusual from the position of traditional benefit-cost analysis (BCA), but it allows the estimate for change in the government surplus, from Eq. (3.13), to resolve the question of the effects on government revenue. The net effect of the NFIP on government income, like other analyses, is the sum of the effects due to the insurance program and the Flood Mitigation Assistance (FMA). Because of this simplicity, the value can be estimated using standard tools from BCA.

7.1 Methodology

Like the other BCA methods presented before, this analysis uses a social surplus method to model the effects of the NFIP's insurance component on government revenues. Beginning with Eq. (3.10), the effect on government revenue from the insurance program includes the ad hocpayments which are represented by a. In brief, the effect on income is the revenue from the NFIP itself minus the administrative fees paid to insurers to administer the program. The values of μ and ζ will be calculated using the same methods as in Sect. 3 and the value of φ is fixed. From before, a can be estimated with κ, the accumulated claims paid by the NFIP, so the final form of ΔG is

J. Howard, II, *Socioeconomic Effects of the National Flood Insurance Program*, SpringerBriefs in Political Science, DOI 10.1007/978-3-319-29063-8_7

$$\Delta G = \mu - \kappa - \varphi\mu - \zeta + a \tag{7.1}$$

$$= \mu - \kappa - \varphi\mu - \zeta + \kappa \tag{7.2}$$

$$= \mu - \varphi\mu - \zeta. \tag{7.3}$$

The value of ΔG is evaluated just as in Chap. 5.

The analysis of the FMA program conducted by the Multihazard Mitigation Council (MMC) includes an estimate of the net effect on government revenue caused by the FMA (Multihazard Mitigation Council 2005, 139–142). The effect on government revenue caused by the FMA is distinct from the net social benefits (NSB) of the FMA program. Instead, the effect on government revenue estimates how much change there is on government revenue for every dollar spent on FMA grants. This estimate, as in the retrospective analysis, is a benefit-cost ratio (BCR) and is $R = 3.65$, or that for every dollar spent on flood mitigation through the FMA program, government revenue will increase by three dollars and 65 cents.

However, unlike in the estimate for the NSB of the FMA program, the authors of the MMC report do not provide information on the statistical distribution of government revenue. For the purposes of the point estimate of the NSB for the FMA and NFIP programs, this does not matter. However, for sensitivity analysis, an estimate of the distribution of the random variable makes stochastic simulation possible. In this instance, it is reasonable to assume the distribution is log-normal, like the NSB to society for the FMA. This is reasonable because of the overlap in contributory statistics between the two estimates and because log-normal distributions naturally arise from the sum of random variables (Limpert et al. 2001).

This does not resolve the question of an appropriate standard deviation for the distribution. The standard deviation for the NSB of the FMA program was found to be 1.1, which suggests a scale though not a value. Absent another value, the value of 1.1 will be used to create a range for sensitivity analysis. Though due to the small effect of the FMA on the change in government revenue, the values of the expected returns to the government do not substantially change the results.

7.2 Estimation Process

The governmental income analysis begins with the county-level financial information which is then aggregated by year, to give a single annualized national figure for premiums, claims, coverage, and grants for the NFIP and FMA. Again, because the aggregation does not span multiple years, there is no need to include any adjustment for inflation. The results of this aggregation are identical to Chap. 5 and are presented in Table 3.6.

Like the other analyses, the last preparatory step is to adjust each year's values to compute the present value as of 2010. This step can be conducted prior to final values for each year provided it is performed consistently across all known values. Because the figures represent historical information, social discounting inflates a particular year's value by the cumulative social discount rate (SDR) since that year. As a result, prior spending increases in value as time goes on. The results of this discounting are also identical to Chap. 5 and are presented in Table 5.2.

At the end of this process, there is a panel dataset representing the annualized estimates of the premiums, claims, coverage, and grants for the NFIP and FMA programs. To this point, this process is identical to the process followed in Chap. 5. The government income change attributable to the insurance program will be calculated using Eq. (7.3):

$$\Delta G = \mu - \varphi\mu - \zeta. \tag{7.4}$$

For the panel dataset, annualized net government revenue change for the NFIP is calculated by applying Eq. (7.3) for each year in the study period which yields the government income estimate for each year. Therefore, the net change in governmental income due to the insurance component of the NFIP from 1996 through 2010 is computable by summing the annualized estimates of the NFIP's change in governmental revenue. These annual changes in government revenue are listed in Table 5.2.

Per the results of Multihazard Mitigation Council (2005, 123), FMA grants produce an increase government revenue and savings of 3.65. This is based on the underlying assumption that the return period for an FMA grant is 50 years and uses an SDR of 2 %. Based on this information, it is possible to estimate an annualized rate of return for the average FMA project by finding the annual rate of return that would yield a return of 3.65 % at a 2 % SDR. The annualized rate of return is 11.62 %, for every year up to 50 years from the grant date. This value does not include any social discounting for future returns, therefore it is necessary to apply social discounting independently of the annualized rate of return. This factor can be used with the previously socially discounted FMA grant amounts to find the net present value of each year's FMA grants over the study period. For the study period, there is 11.62 % returns for every year after the grant is made until 2010. Estimates are provided in Table 7.1.

The returns column of Table 7.1 shows a decreasing revenue in later years. The point estimates of the revenue change for the FMA program are created by summing the revenue for each year for each panel dataset. Because of the bias against later projects, the cumulative ΔG for the FMA projects is substantially negative. This data presentation and calculation issue can be alleviated by examining the long-term returns to the FMA program. Using the original estimate of the BCR for the FMA programs developed by Rose et al. (2007), the 50-year return on the FMA can be calculated. Using the BCR of 3.65, the ΔG of the FMA through the year 2060 can be calculated. This BCR assumes an SDR of 2 %.

Following the calculation of sums of the ΔG for the NFIP and FMA components of the analysis, the final step is to aggregate the results to create a point estimate of the change in government revenue due to the NFIP and FMA programs. The sum of the NFIP ΔG is 35 billion dollars in both 2010 and forecast to 2060. This is because there is no change over time to non-FMA components. However, for the

Table 7.1 FMA grant returns by year (2010 dollars)

Year	Grants	Returns	Revenue
1996	1,767,983	205,360	−1,562,624
1997	21,492,157	2,689,308	−18,802,849
1998	25,242,848	5,479,411	−19,763,438
1999	23,230,527	7,903,461	−15,327,066
2000	26,009,597	10,465,189	−15,544,407
2001	17,812,281	12,015,069	−5,797,213
2002	14,648,051	13,166,392	−1,481,659
2003	16,167,162	14,544,648	−1,622,514
2004	23,994,971	16,731,359	−7,263,612
2005	22,320,305	18,648,406	−3,671,898
2006	26,790,631	20,913,083	−5,877,548
2007	30,615,438	23,526,408	−7,089,030
2008	112,898,610	35,754,035	−77,144,574
2009	124,892,141	49,147,906	−75,744,235
2010	72,689,815	55,993,690	−16,696,124

Table 7.2 Expected distributions of factors in the government revenue analysis

Variable	Distribution	Specifications
φ	Uniform	Range: [0.15 − 0.17]
R	Log-normal	Mean: 3.65; Std. dev.: 1.1

FMA program, the sum of the ΔG is −273 million dollars in 2010 and in 2060, it is 2 billion dollars. These sum to 34.57 billion dollars in 2010 and 36.89 billion dollars in 2060.

7.3 Sensitivity Analysis

Because each of the component factors in this analysis consists of a point estimate, there is a potential for statistical error to corrupt the final result. Sensitivity analysis provides an opportunity to analyze the errors involved and test the statistical assumptions included in the analysis.

This analysis will use two methods of sensitivity analysis to understand the effects on government revenue. The first will be to calculate an estimate excluding the year 2005, to remove the high-effect year which included Hurricanes Katrina and Rita. Second, this analysis will also use Monte Carlo simulation (MCS) with simultaneous uncertainty to understand the effects of the NFIP and FMA programs on government revenue (Boardman et al. 2010, 183–187). For this analysis, the sensitivity analysis will consist of a stochastic simulation over the input variables described in Table 7.2. These two variables are the core variables in the analysis where the values are estimated from other data, rather than being known a priori.

The first variable to be analyzed during the sensitivity analysis is φ, the Write Your Own (WYO) fee to insurers. This can range from 15 to 17 %. This will also be simulated using a uniform distribution. The second variable to be analyzed as part of the sensitivity analysis is R, the BCR of the FMA program grants. This uses the presumed log-normal distribution established as part of this analysis and assumes a standard deviation of that distribution of 1.1.

This analysis will show how the change in government revenue responds to changes in the environment surrounding the NFIP, in particular how returns are yielded from FMA grants. This will inform the analysis and help explain the uncertainty of the results. There are two major ways a sensitivity analysis can contribute to understanding this result. One centers on the effect of Hurricane Katrina, which caused significant damage along the Gulf Coast of the USA. The second focuses on MCS, testing the assumptions and the net validity of the results under stress.

Following the calculation of sums of the ΔG for the NFIP and FMA components of the analysis, the final step is to aggregate the results to create a point estimate of the change in government revenue due to the NFIP and FMA programs. The sum of the NFIP ΔG is 33 billion dollars in both 2010 and forecast to 2060. This is because there is no change over time to non-FMA components. However, the sum of ΔG is −270 million dollars in 2010 and in the 2060, it is 2 billion dollars for the FMA program. These sum to 32 billion dollars in 2010 and 35 billion dollars in 2060.

The MCS of the NFIP's effect on government revenue is useful to understand the implications of the program for both taxpayers and policymakers. In particular, this analysis makes a number of assumptions about the degree and type of effects various aspects of the NFIP and FMA programs have on government revenues and the tax systems. These assumptions are distributions for the components of the program and are given in Table 7.3. Each of these assumptions is based on measured effect levels and is subject to sensitivity concerns. In contrast, other values such as the amount of claims paid into the NFIP or the value of grants given as part of the FMA are assumed to be static given the nature of this analysis. This is due to the retrospective orientation of the analysis. A prospective analysis would also include sensitivity analysis focusing on the possible flood damages and potential changes in participation patterns, as well as changes in grant-making patterns by Federal Emergency Management Agency (FEMA).

The sensitivity analysis yields a mean NFIP ΔG of 34.6 billion dollars in 2010 (s.d. 0.245). There are 100 % positive trials from the MCS. Similarly, the analysis yields a mean NFIP ΔG of 36.9 billion dollars in 2060 (s.d. 0.311). There are 100 %

Table 7.3 Sensitivity analysis parameters

Variable	Description	Distribution	Parameters
ϕ	Administrative fee rate	Uniform	Lower bound: 0.15; Upper bound: 0.17
FMA BCR	FMA return rate	Log-normal	Mean: 3.6; Standard deviation: 1.1

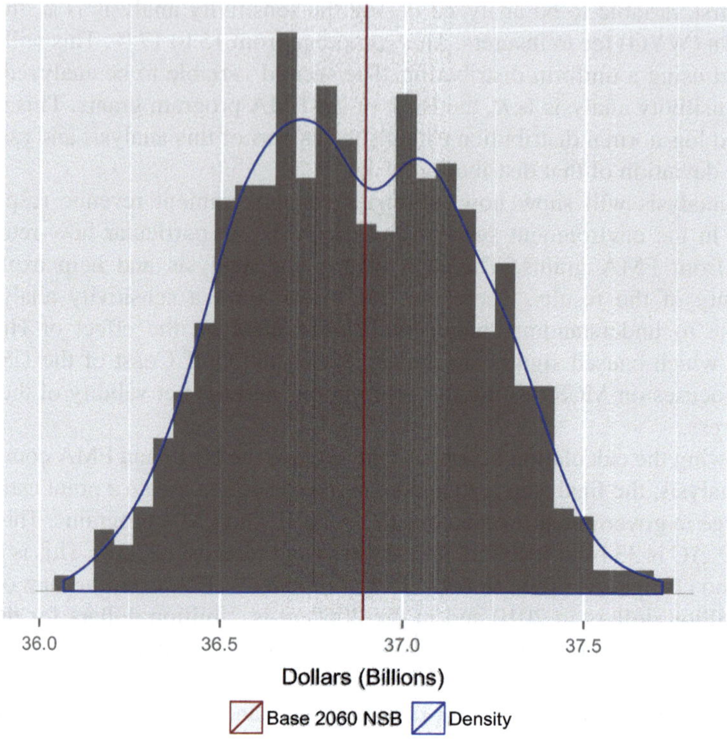

Fig. 7.1 Histogram of government revenue sensitivity analysis outcomes for (year 2060)

positive trials from the MCS. In addition to these summarized results, a histogram showing the distribution of ΔG is provided in Fig. 7.1.

Finally, two figures showing the sensitivity of the BCA are available. The first, Fig. 7.2, shows the sensitivity of the change in government revenue to the amount of fees paid to insurance providers to administer the program on behalf of the NFIP. Second, Fig. 7.3, shows the sensitivity of the change in government revenues to the effects of the FMA on government revenues.

7.4 Discussion and Conclusions

The hypothesis test is given by,

H_0: The net present value of the distributional effect of the NFIP on the US government from 1996 through 2010 were less than or equal to zero (0)

H_1: The net present value of the distributional effect of the NFIP on the US government from 1996 through 2010 were greater than zero (0)

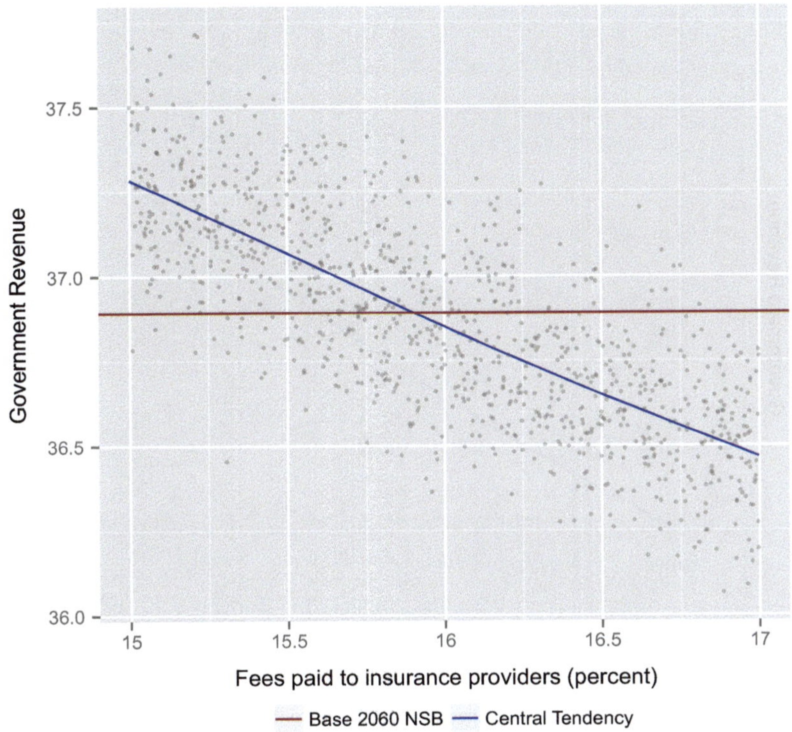

Fig. 7.2 Government revenue sensitivity to changes in administrative fees (year 2060)

The results of the base analysis and sensitivity analyses are given in Table 7.4. The results are positive across each of the analyses, showing the positive returns to the government from the NFIP and FMA programs. The NFIP and FMA programs have a strong positive effect on government revenues, since the costs of flood recovery are shifted, at least in part, to the premiums paid by homeowners to the NFIP. The remaining amount is projected based on reductions in losses on flooding and other expected gains resulting from the mitigation grant. MCS of these results shows there is a relatively narrow band of potential outcomes for government revenue from the NFIP and FMA programs. There are between 36.07 billion dollars and 37.71 billion dollars (spread over 50 years) in savings to the federal government due to the NFIP and FMA programs for the study period. The spread of these potential outcomes is approximately 4.77 % of the point estimate for the change in government revenue. As a result, the estimates created by the simulation provide a positive effect on governmental revenues across the entire spread of potential values for estimated model parameters.

As only two variables contribute to the government revenue model that are not explicitly determined by the finances of the NFIP, only two variables contribute to the sensitivity analysis. The first variable, the amount of fees paid by the NFIP to

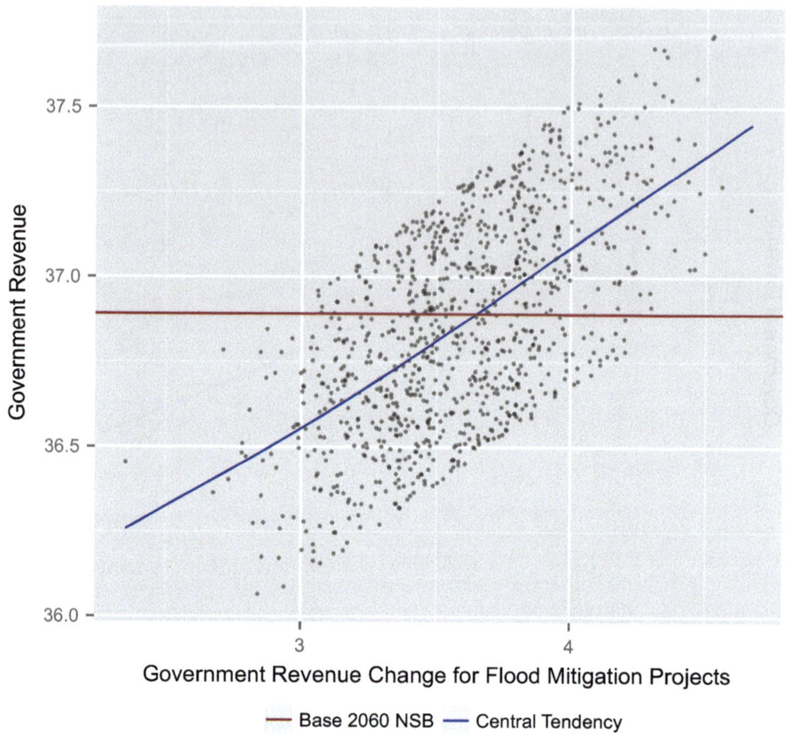

Fig. 7.3 Government revenue sensitivity to changes in the FMA returns (year 2060)

Table 7.4 Summary of government revenue results (billions of dollars)

Value in year	2010	Forecast to 2060
Base analysis	34.57	36.89
Excluding 2005	32.33	34.56
Sensitivity analysis mean	34.57	36.87

private insurers to administer the program, has a small but clearly defined effect. In a conventional BCA, this sort of transfer is considered a wash and would be ignored. However, this analysis removes all non-federal government actors from standing and the loss to the government must be considered while the benefit to insurers must not be. Because the range of fees paid is bounded between 15 and 17 % of the premiums paid into the program, the fees will reduce revenues, but at a defined and limited rate. The sensitivity of the government revenue to the administrative fee rate is shown in Fig. 7.2.

The second effect variable to contribute to the governmental revenue model is the returns to FMA programs. The historical FMA grants are set and grants are historically limited to a fixed amount, and were at most 40 million dollars per year during the study period, and the funding comes directly from the premiums the

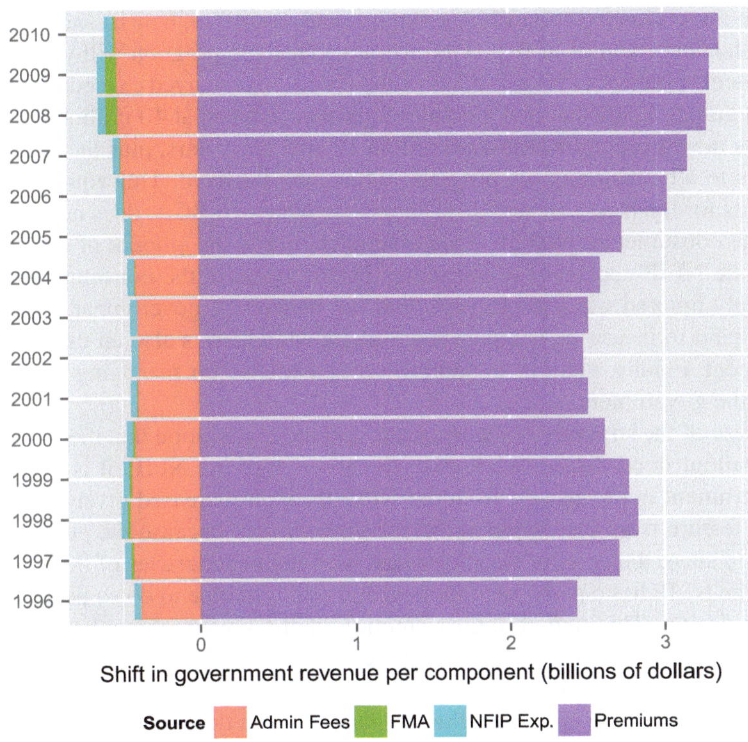

Fig. 7.4 Tornado plot of government revenues by year

NFIP generates. Because the NFIP produces substantially more in premiums than 40 million dollars, the expenses of the FMA program are less than the fees paid to insurers, overall. Further, these expenses generate new revenue to the government through prevented tax losses and other expenses. Since the returns to the government are log-normally distributed, the change in government revenue due to the FMA tends to cluster near the lower end of the range in a sensitivity analysis. However, a log-normal distribution has a long and narrow tail, permitting higher returns. The sensitivity of the government revenue to the FMA returns is shown in Fig. 7.3.

The effects of programs and components are shown in Fig. 7.4. Because the effects on government revenues are narrowly bounded, it is possible to bind the entire effect. Beginning with Eq. (7.3), the effects of the FMA can be added directly to get the complete change in government revenue. Provided this sum is greater than 0, the government will see an increase in revenue,

$$0 < \Delta S + (R - 1)M, \tag{7.5}$$

where R is the change in government revenue caused by the FMA program and M is the amount of grants made under the FMA program. In the pathological case where there are no returns from the FMA program (and, therefore, $R = 0$) and all insurers receive the maximum of 17 % in administrative fees, the program will yield positive government revenues as long as 83 % of the premiums received exceeds the amount made in grants. Since the total amount of grants is capped at 40 million dollars per year, this means premiums must exceed 48.19 million dollars, plus the government expenses to administering the program, which are not fixed. This equation, unlike the results for the base case and distributionally weighted BCA, does not depend on either the consumer surplus for flood insurance, nor is the amount of claims made against the NFIP necessary to calculate. This is because the consumer surplus is completely ignored when the surplus does not benefit the government. In addition, the fees paid to insurance companies are included, which is also an expense to the government. Finally, there is an administrative expense for managing the program paid by the government.

Because of the structure of the program, and the assumption that the government would bailout flood disaster victims in the absence of the NFIP, it is unlikely for the government not to benefit from the NFIP through increased revenue. This is a positive feature from the standpoint of the government, because the purpose of the NFIP is to share the costs of flood disasters with the beneficiaries of flood recovery funds. The NFIP has clearly met that goal and will continue to do so because of the program design. This underlying assumption of the government's behavior if the NFIP did not exist remains subject to further research.

However, despite these results, the NFIP and FMA programs are not necessarily the most cost effective option for the government. The debts incurred by the NFIP are not included in this analysis. Those debts are nominally held by the Treasury, and from a governmental revenue perspective, cancel each other out. However, if the government lacks sufficient funds to loan to the NFIP, the Treasury must borrow on the capital markets to provide access to funding. The effects of this borrowing are not included in this analysis. Further, the NFIP's debts may be so large as to indicate insolvency absent a policy change or direct bailout. Such a bailout would not eliminate the positive governmental income found in this analysis, but it is clear evidence of the NFIP's inability to be self-sufficient in the current policy environment.

The implications of this are significant since the NFIP and FMA programs have some economic and social costs. Based on the results of Chap. 6, if the government is increasing its revenue, it is doing so at the social costs of lower economic classes. But this also reflects who participates in the program and at what rates. This may not be the case, though; as Bin et al. (2011) has shown, the wealthier individuals tend to pay slightly more into the program than they receive, versus others.

This analysis does not take into consideration non-NFIP response to flood disasters, such as funding for noninsureds, including the federal government itself, as well as emergency response activities, such as evacuations. In this regard, the costs and benefits to the federal government are not captured completely in this analysis. Nevertheless, this analysis shows that the NFIP and FMA programs jointly contribute to increase governmental revenues. This analysis also provides a template for analyzing governmental income under other disaster management programs such for as earthquakes or terrorism. Governments at all levels often act as last-resort insurers for drivers, financial institutions, and other private needs, beyond natural disasters. Understanding the implications on government revenue from these programs provides a critical tool for evaluation of policy changes.

Chapter 8
Conclusions

The four evaluations included in this book have provided an integrated picture of the net social benefits (NSB) from the National Flood Insurance Program (NFIP) and Flood Mitigation Assistance (FMA) programs. Overall, this picture is about the interaction between the consumer surplus for the NFIP, the marginal excess tax burden (METB) for taxes not collected to fund ad hocflood recovery if the NFIP exists, and the change in government revenues. The NSB of the NFIP are positive because of this interaction, but as the sensitivity analysis shows, the results remain positive even if one of these elements is removed from the economic model of the programs. However, this conclusion is predicated upon the initial analytical assumptions outlined in Sect. 1.3.

These benefits accrue across actor categories, but not necessarily equitably. Producers do not gain from this program. However, that is because the economic model assumes producers, the insurance companies, provide administrative support to implement the NFIP to the government at cost. The fee paid to producers is a fixed fee and if a producer can provide administrative support at a cost less than the fee, producers would benefit from the difference. But even without those prospective benefits to producers, the NSB is positive.

Consumers benefit more than other groups, though this benefit is not a direct transfer. The consumer benefit comes from the implied difference between the general consumer's willingness-to-pay (WTP) for flood insurance and the actual premium rates they pay to the NFIP for the service. The consumer surplus for the NFIP is estimated at 791 dollars per policy in 2010 dollars. The estimate is roughly double the amount policyholders should expect to pay for flood insurance and suggests that policyholders receive substantial benefit from the NFIP if they are not required to be policyholders by the mortgage requirement. This is despite the relatively lower numbers of policyholders outside the 100-year floodplain.

The consumer surplus found in this analysis may overstate the benefit received by all program participants. A substantial number of program participants drop out of the program after only a few years suggesting they receive no benefit from

J. Howard, II, *Socioeconomic Effects of the National Flood Insurance Program*,
SpringerBriefs in Political Science, DOI 10.1007/978-3-319-29063-8_8

participating. If this is the case, the NSB found is overstated, but would remain positive even if the consumer surplus from the flood insurance program alone were zero. However, if there is a positive consumer surplus for the NFIP, the simplest approach to increase the NSB of the program would be to increase program participation. This would increase the total number of policies in force and drive up the total NSB by increasing the combined consumer surplus per policy. The NFIP was changed substantially in 2012 following Hurricane Sandy. Those changes had pushed the program to reduce the subsidy and increase participation, though many were rolled back following policyholder objections.

Those same policyholders, however, have substantially offset the costs of the government to provide flood recovery. This is the source of the governmental benefits found in this analysis. The government income change due to the NFIP and FMA programs is positive. This supports the original goals of the NFIP, which were to, at least partially, shift the costs of flood recovery to the principal beneficiaries of flood recovery. This shift has reduced the overall burden of flooding on taxpayers. In this respect, the NFIP has been a success, regardless of its broader social and economic effects.

The last group of effects is the externalities caused by the NFIP. There is a large benefit to the economy as a whole from not using tax revenue to fund flood recovery. Therefore, the NSB of the NFIP and FMA programs increases if the NFIP exists. The METB estimate provides this element of the economic model for the programs. However, the estimate assumes the government's ad hocflood relief funding would be equivalent to the amount of claims paid by the NFIP under the insurance plan. This assumption may not be valid since the government may choose not to provide ad hocflood relief following some disasters or may provide less or more relief than the insurance program does. The sensitivity analysis provided here tests the importance of this assumption and finds there is still a positive NSB even if the METB from ad hocflood relief were not counted.

As a result, the NSB increases as the NFIP pays greater claims. The NSB shifts downward when the year 2005 is removed from the estimate, removing the effect of Hurricanes Katrina and Rita. When those larger flood events are removed from consideration, the NSB of the programs is positive, but lower in current terms because of the lost positive benefit of the missing METB for claims and the missing consumer surplus for the year. This implies that the NSB for the NFIP increases with more and larger disasters. This counter-intuitive conclusion stems from the understanding that the NFIP is a response to flood disasters and that flood disasters would occur whether the NFIP existed, the federal government provides ad hocflood recovery, or some other flood recovery regime were in place. Therefore, the benefit comes from not using taxes to pay for whatever flood recovery regime in place.

In addition to the METB, the other large externality is the environmental effect of the NFIP. This analysis does not include the environmental effects from either ad hocflood recovery or the NFIP. Under the assumption that ad hocflood relief is identical to the claims paid by the NFIP, the environmental effects would also be identical. However, differences in the government's response if the NFIP did not exist from the NFIP's behavior could change the net environmental effect. If the environmental effect is more negative than the environmental effect without the NFIP, then there is an externality loss missing from the sufficient statistic. The loss would decrease the NSB of the programs and if large enough, may change the sign of the results. A better understanding of the environmental effects of flood recovery, coupled with a national-level model to estimate the dollar value of the environmental effects, is necessary.

The distributional analysis shows that the benefits realized by the NFIP and FMA programs disproportionately accrue to wealthier areas within the USA. When analyzed and weighted for distributional analysis, the decreasing weights for wealthier jurisdictions reduced their contribution to the NSB versus the increasing weights for less wealthy jurisdictions. As the spread between the weights for wealthy and less wealthy jurisdictions increased, the NSB for the programs decreased. Based on this evidence, the programs' benefits are accruing to wealthier jurisdictions more than less wealthy. Therefore, the program is regressive in the sense that money to pay for benefits is coming from those with fewer resources and claims are being paid to those with greater resource.

In a sense, the NFIP rests in an approximate equilibrium where short-term costs are balanced in the benefit-cost analysis (BCA) with older large claim years and future returns from flood mitigation being inflated by social discounting. The sample period is 16 years and the bright line for flood planning is the 100-year return period. The difference between the two means during the sample period is relatively short, but still exhibits both large and small loss years. Whether the sample is representative is important. For instance, the balancing act may be disturbed by climate change-driven changes to the floodplain and flood events, but will be difficult to predict as the changes to flood patterns are not yet predictable. Despite these concerns, the program has proved advantageous to taxpayers, and the economy generally, by partially shifting the costs of rebuilding following a flood to the beneficiaries.

8.1 Policy Implications

The place of the NFIP in the complete insurance picture is striking. The NFIP does not compete directly with private insurance firms since private insurers do not offer primary flood insurance (Marlett 1997, 139). Due to the NFIP's Write Your Own (WYO) program structure, private insurers manage the specifics of insurance policy implementation and the NFIP scores well on insurance industry benchmarks, such as expense ratio (Marlett 1997, 137). The NFIP is not subject to either dividend payments or taxation and the program can build its reserve against losses unimpeded by profit concerns, because it is an agency of the US government.

While the program provides a net benefit to society and saves the government money, those benefits come at a cost of moderately regressive distributional effects. Wealthier counties are benefiting from the program at the expense of poorer counties when the distributional effects are evaluated nationally. The sociological costs of these benefits should be evaluated and changes to the NFIP should consider the sociological costs of the proposed change. Evaluation of proposed changes should also consider the net cost to government.

The potential addition of wind insurance to the NFIP raises economic issues similar to those posed by floods-only coverage. This issue is important because hurricanes and other severe wind events can occur concurrently with flood events. A proposed addition of wind insurance policies to the NFIP raises concerns with direct competition against private insurers.

Altering the NFIP to insure against multiple perils might improve the NSB of the program, and can reduce net risk. Insuring against multiple perils is how private insurers reduce their net risk against losses stemming from a single event (McMillan 2008). However, this multiple peril strategy is only effective if those perils are uncorrelated. The combination of wind and flood damage from superstorms or hurricanes is a significant threat to the financial viability of a combined program. Wind coverage is unlikely to reduce the NFIP's net risk exposure. No detailed analysis of an integrated program is conducted here but wind coverage is an area of potential research.

Another option to reduce an outstanding risk position, used by reinsurers, is to use geographic dispersion of risk (Cutler and Zeckhauser 1999), which is effective because it is less likely that it would flood in different regions at the same time. This is complex because the NFIP is a nationwide program and is inherently geographically dispersed. But in practice, the policy that federally regulated mortgage granting institutions require flood insurance for mortgages on properties on the floodplain coupled with the breadth of the floodplain along the Gulf Coast means more than 40 % of all NFIP policies are located in Florida (Michel-Kerjan and Kousky 2010). A broader requirement for purchasing flood insurance or a reduction in building in Florida's floodplain would be necessary for the NFIP to gain the advantages inherent in being a nationwide program.

Kunreuther and Michel-Kerjan (2010), in a related essay, address the question of insuring against natural catastrophes. They propose long-term contracts for managing long-term insurance risk (Kunreuther and Michel-Kerjan 2010). The authors note that some natural disasters, such as the 500-year flood, are outside the decision-making time frame, or so unlikely, that the average homeowner cannot realistically measure the risk associated with the event. Long-term contracts, instead of 1 year renewable policies, can help homeowners manage the risk by placing a long-term outlook on the matter. The authors select the NFIP as an obvious place to test long-term insurance due to the simpler political environment, a lack of state regulators, and the natural leveling of the average risk profile associated with flooding, when addressed at the national level.

8.2 Directions for Future Research

A number of directions for future research are worth exploring. One avenue for future research centers on the distributionally weighted analysis of the NSB. Due to limitations of data and the manner in which grants are awarded by Federal Emergency Management Agency (FEMA), this analysis was limited in the county-level distributional analysis. As significant between county differences in wealth and income exist, finer detail in assigning state-level grants to local jurisdictions would increase the detail of distributionally weighted results.

From a public finance perspective, it is important to maximize the NSB of any program. Future research could use this analysis to model the NFIP and FMA programs and alter the parameters of the programs to find the optimal NSB. However, maximizing the NSB of the programs may come with distributional effects larger than the effects under the current program. Therefore, additional research should also include the distributional weighted model of the NFIP and FMA programs' social surplus.

In addition, this evaluation relied on research into the consumer surplus of the NFIP. This estimate for the consumer surplus has a number of limitations, including the broad categorization of program participants and the concentration of survey respondents along the coasts. Recent research by Botzen et al. (2008) has shown the effectiveness of large scale contingent valuation method (CVM) surveys for understanding the consumer surplus for flood insurance in the Netherlands. It is reasonable to execute a similar survey in the USA to assess the consumer surplus for flood insurance under the conditions imposed by the NFIP.

From a behavioral economics perspective, one research area focuses on how perceptions of risk change after a major flood event. Practically speaking, this is the question of whether or not policyholders change purchasing patterns after nearby floods. If patterns change, this might reflect changes in the consumer surplus for flood insurance, changing the NSB of the NFIP.

A related area to explore focuses on risk management from a game theory perspective. If potential policyholders do not join the program, they may assume the government will provide other flood recovery assistance, without direct charge. This is akin to the free rider problem, since some policyholders have opted into to the program. Without a functioning market for primary flood insurance, a market clearing price is not established and potentially non-rational decision-making is indirectly supported by the NFIP pricing structure.

Looking forward, the NFIP and FMA programs face obstacles caused by global climate change. This analysis does not explicitly allow for the effects of climate change. However, the effects of climate change that are responsible for specific insurance gains and losses are included as those gains and losses are realized. The historical results should not be used to estimate prospective gains or losses as prospective gains or losses would not account for the ongoing effects of climate change. Future research should estimate the effects to climate change on the NFIP and determine how to predict forward-looking NSB for the NFIP.

Other proposals to consider include giving FEMA, through the NFIP, the ability to restrict floodplain development by purchasing land and dedicating it as open space. Barnhizer (2003) advocates using federal funds to compensate existing landowners and targeting properties deemed high-risk or environmentally sensitive for the program. Through such a program, the net risk to the NFIP could be reduced. However, it is worth noting that FEMA already has the power to purchase some repetitive loss properties rather than sustaining continued losses. Other proposals to reduce floodplain development through market action have been proposed, as well (Titus 1998). As the change in the environment is unaddressed here, quantifying the effects of ecological damage from the NFIP is a topic for investigation.

In other areas of risk management, this method could be applied to similar disaster insurance programs in other jurisdictions. For instance, other counties maintain similar flood insurance programs. Other hazards may also be so analyzed: California maintains an earthquake insurance program with a similar compulsory aspect that could be similarly analyzed. Finally, analysis of Louisiana Citizens Property Insurance Corporation or the Maryland Automobile Insurance Fund, both insurers of last resort, may be conducted similarly, to examine their benefit to society.

8.3 Final Remarks

The NFIP and FMA programs are complex and involve many interactions. These interactions can be complex, especially when the effects of distributional weighting are included. The long run risk of flooding is still poorly understood despite several decades of study by FEMA. Environmental changes such as climate change and geoengineering also change the flood risk. Because of these changes, an analysis like this is only a point estimate representing the NSB of the program at a single time.

Still, BCA is a powerful tool for analyzing public policy programs. With BCA, the NSB of a program can be identified with some degree of certainty. However, no analysis is ever complete and this analysis is no exception. There is much more work possible to gain a deeper knowledge from more accurate estimates of damages and the risk associated with flooding. It is also possible to gain better estimates of the consumer surplus for flood insurance. Changes to the program also require new analysis to understand.

This evaluation has provided a first comprehensive BCA of the NFIP, but it should not be the last. Revisions and updates to the economic model should be pursued and encouraged. An entirely different analytical approach could also be used to test the results. Regardless, understanding the NFIP is important from a public policy perspective and can provide better policy solutions to the public and policymakers.

Appendix A
Timeline of Federal Flood Insurance

1956	The Federal Flood Insurance Act of 1956 (FFIA) creates a pilot federal flood insurance program
1968	The National Flood Insurance Act of 1968 (NFIA) establishes the NFIP
1973	The Flood Disaster Protection Act of 1973 (FDPA) mandates flood insurance for high-risk properties securing a mortgage from a federally regulated institution
1974	The Disaster Relief Act of 1974 (DRA) creates a mechanism for handling disasters and emergencies at the federal level
1979	Executive Order 12127 (EO 12127) transfers authority over the NFIP to the FEMA
1982	The Coastal Barrier Resources Act of 1982 (CBRA) reduces availability of insurance for new and improved properties
1989	NFIP losses from Hurricane Hugo exceed 375 million dollars
1993	Midwest Floods cause more than 270 million dollars in claims against the NFIP
1994	The National Flood Insurance Reform Act of 1994 (NFIRA) creates the FMA program with a goal of reducing claims under the NFIP
2004	The Flood Insurance Reform Act of 2004 (FIRA) aims to reduce repetitive losses on high-risk properties

J. Howard, II, *Socioeconomic Effects of the National Flood Insurance Program*, SpringerBriefs in Political Science, DOI 10.1007/978-3-319-29063-8

2005	NFIP losses from all hurricanes, including Katrina, exceed 17 billion dollars
2008	The Flood Insurance Reform and Modernization Act of 2008 (FIRMA), to extend the NFIP to provide wind coverage, is passed by Congress but vetoed by the President
2010	The Flood Insurance Reform Priorities Act of 2010 (FIRPA), to reauthorize the NFIP and increase maximum coverage, is passed by the House of Representatives and currently pending before the Senate
2012	Hurricane Sandy causes 7.9 billion dollars in losses to the NFIP
2013	The Biggert-Waters Flood Insurance Reform Act raises rates to reflect true risk

Appendix B
Principal Data Sources

This appendix includes data from the primary data sources used in calculating the benefits and costs of the NFIP. Tables B.1 and B.2 both show a representative sample, selected at random, of FEMA Dataset A and FEMA Dataset B, respectively. The small sample was chosen to provide a sense of the data and its structure, without including the entire dataset. FEMA Dataset A is 91,528 rows and FEMA Dataset B is 31,307 rows. Each sample shown is 20 rows.

FEMA Dataset B is roughly a third of the size of the FEMA Dataset A because FEMA Dataset B represents only claims information. Both datasets provide information about the NFIP with key columns represent the state, county, and year, with the actual program data represented as addition columns. For FEMA Dataset B, if there were no claims within a given county during a given year, then a row is omitted, rather than provided with empty or zero value entries.

The following table of fiscal year consumer price index values was created by averaging monthly Consumer Price Index (CPI) figures for the October–September period of each year.

The following table of fiscal year government borrowing rates was created by averaging monthly borrowing figures for the October–September period of each year. This table also includes a column "sdr2010" which is the associated discount rate, based on federal borrowing rates, that can be used for social discounting. The construction and use of this table are similar to the CPI constructed by Bureau of Labor Statistics (BLS). However, the base year (that is, where the value is 100) is chosen to be 2011. From here, it is possible to socially discount an amount from any year to any other year by multiplying by the ratio of source to target year.

Table B.3 provides a representative sample, selected at random, of FEMA Dataset C. FEMA Dataset C is 2107 rows. The sample size shown in the table is, again, 20 rows (Tables B.4 and B.5).

J. Howard, II, *Socioeconomic Effects of the National Flood Insurance Program*, SpringerBriefs in Political Science, DOI 10.1007/978-3-319-29063-8

Table B.1 Sample data from FEMA Dataset A

state	state_code	county	county_code	year	pif	cif	coverage	premiums
KANSAS	20	COFFEY COUNTY	31	2002	20	20	1627	12632
ILLINOIS	17	MONTGOMERY COUNTY	135	1981	10	10	208	1716
VIRGINIA	51	SALEM, INDEPENDENT CITY OF	775	1986	346	346	22535	126935
OKLAHOMA	40	TULSA COUNTY	143	2001	1618	1618	162831	737643
MICHIGAN	26	IONIA COUNTY	67	2006	124	124	12480	74034
PENNSYLVANIA	42	LYCOMING COUNTY	81	1999	2563	2563	176837	1339481
ARKANSAS	5	POPE COUNTY	115	2004	164	164	16868	92019
LOUISIANA	22	ST. JOHN THE BAPTIST PARISH	95	2001	4847	4847	664459	1662093
INDIANA	18	KOSCIUSKO COUNTY	85	2001	768	768	63619	302866
FLORIDA	12	GULF COUNTY	45	1998	1258	1254	139995	539935
TEXAS	48	CARSON COUNTY	65	1989	4	4	132	970
GEORGIA	13	BULLOCH COUNTY	31	1998	223	223	23845	86082
VIRGINIA	51	ALEXANDRIA, INDEPENDENT CITY O	510	1998	1352	407	145842	296831
GEORGIA	13	GILMER COUNTY	123	2007	294	283	63449	203740
KANSAS	20	HARVEY COUNTY	79	1980	556	556	14822	38343
TEXAS	48	HIDALGO COUNTY	215	2006	7643	7643	1285587	2694102
PENNSYLVANIA	42	CAMBRIA COUNTY	21	1987	2567	2567	132929	754922
WEST VIRGINIA	54	SUMMERS COUNTY	89	2004	242	242	15418	98539
TEXAS	48	GILLESPIE COUNTY	171	1979	25	25	749	2182
INDIANA	18	SCOTT COUNTY	143	2000	46	46	4751	25773

Table B.2 Sample data from FEMA Dataset B

state	year	county	num_claims	pay_bldg	pay_cont	pay_icc
GEORGIA	1985	CHATHAM COUNTY	14	26268.91	13590.85	0.00
SOUTH DAKOTA	2002	DAY COUNTY	2	55716.91	447.81	0.00
MINNESOTA	2001	OTTER TAIL COUNTY	10	25875.29	408.15	0.00
NEW YORK	1996	BRONX COUNTY	332	2427360.78	2333665.01	0.00
KENTUCKY	1992	MERCER COUNTY	1	3684.72	0.00	0.00
FLORIDA	1997	OSCEOLA COUNTY	4	15052.22	209.50	0.00
OHIO	1981	LAKE COUNTY	45	220968.85	38761.70	0.00
INDIANA	2010	OWEN COUNTY	1	6303.66	0.00	0.00
MISSOURI	1979	CAPE GIRARDEAU COUNTY	68	176766.05	98187.72	0.00
ALABAMA	1983	BALDWIN COUNTY	34	87097.07	30418.68	0.00
TEXAS	1991	TYLER COUNTY	2	11570.82	0.00	0.00
NEW JERSEY	2005	BURLINGTON COUNTY	21	162643.83	18117.22	0.00
TEXAS	2003	STARR COUNTY	3	28535.38	5900.38	0.00
TEXAS	2001	HARRIS COUNTY	20165	640148199.00	217353127.10	3624833.24
KENTUCKY	1981	PIKE COUNTY	145	633698.08	506063.21	0.00
CALIFORNIA	2009	SAN MATEO COUNTY	1	0.00	95665.34	0.00
MINNESOTA	2002	BECKER COUNTY	1	16536.28	0.00	0.00
GEORGIA	2005	GWINNETT COUNTY	6	62315.97	7057.39	0.00
ALASKA	1994	FAIRBANKS DIVISION	3	13060.97	5271.70	0.00
FLORIDA	2002	COLLIER COUNTY	2	13975.09	2750.13	0.00

Table B.3 Sample data from FEMA Dataset C

state	state_code	county	county_code	subgrantee	program	year	amount
Washington	53	King	33	Snoqualmie, City Of	FMA	2001	167670.00
Mississippi	28	Grenada	43	Grenada, City Of	FMA	1998	48479.00
New Jersey	34	–	–	State of New Jersey Dept. of Environmental Protection: Green Acres Program	FMA	2011	3562500.00
Massachusetts	25	–	23	Town of Hull	FMA	2009	240899.28
Utah	49	Cache	5	Logan, City Of	FMA	2000	93240.00
New Jersey	34	Mercer	21	Ewing, Township Of	FMA	1998	2283.00
New Hampshire	33	–	15	Town of Londonderry	SRL	2010	109699.56
Oregon	41	–	67	Washington County	FMA	2008	57638.68
Texas	48	–	439	City of Arlington	RFC	2008	2031107.00
Florida	12	Statewide	117	Citrus County *	FMA	1997	56226.69
Texas	48	–	245	Jefferson County Waterway and Navigational District	FMA	2006	35876.13
Colorado	8	Otero	89	La Junta, City Of	FMA	1997	79944.00
Florida	12	–	101	City of Port Richey	FMA	2005	162974.50
Louisiana	22	–	113	Vermilion Parish Police Jury	SRL	2011	176445.00
California	6	–	71	City of Redlands	FMA	2006	14691.00
Illinois	17	Henry	73	Cleveland, Village Of	FMA	2000	285000.00
Kentucky	21	Christian	47	Hopkinsville, City Of	FMA	2000	32839.00
Florida	12	–	31	City of Jacksonville	FMA	2005	26833.46
New Jersey	34	Statewide	–	Statewide	FMA	1998	9595.33
Florida	12	–	75	Town of Yankeetown	FMA	2004	181284.75

Table B.4 Fiscal year CPI measures

Year	fycpi
1996	155.62
1997	159.78
1998	162.38
1999	165.50
2000	170.76
2001	176.26
2002	178.90
2003	183.10
2004	187.35
2005	193.51
2006	200.63
2007	205.34
2008	214.46
2009	213.77
2010	217.37
2011	223.14

Table B.5 Fiscal year SDR rates

Year	Rate	sdr2010
1996	6.33	196.02
1997	6.46	184.12
1998	5.57	174.40
1999	5.27	165.67
2000	6.17	156.04
2001	5.22	148.30
2002	4.80	141.51
2003	3.95	136.14
2004	4.30	130.52
2005	4.21	125.25
2006	4.76	119.56
2007	4.72	114.17
2008	3.92	109.87
2009	3.21	106.45
2010	3.36	102.99
2011	2.99	100.00

References

Anderson PS (2006) Floodplain development and considerations for better national policies. Master's Thesis, South Dakota State University

Arnold JL (1988) The evolution of the 1936 Flood Control Act. United States Army Corps of Engineers, Fort Belvoir

Atkinson AB (1970) On the measurement of economic inequality. J Econ Theory 3(2):244–263

Barnhizer DD (2003) Givings recapture: funding public acquisition of private property interests on the coasts. Harv Environ Law Rev 27:295–375

Bin O, Polasky S (2004) Effects of flood hazards on property values: evidence before and after Hurricane Floyd. Land Econ 80(4):490–500

Bin O, Kruse JB, Landry CE (2008) Flood hazards, insurance rates, and amenities: evidence from the coastal housing market. J Risk Insur 75(1):63–82

Bin O, Bishop JA, Kousky C (2011) Redistributional effects of the National Flood Insurance Program. Technical Report DP 11-14, Washington

Bingham K, Charron M, Kirschner G, Messick R, Sabade S (2006) The role of actuarial soundness in the National Flood Insurance Program. Deloitte Consulting and American Institutes for Research, Washington

Boardman AE, Greenberg DH, Vining AR, Weimer DL (2010) Cost-benefit analysis: concepts and practice, 4th edn. Pearson series in economics. Prentice Hall, Upper Saddle River

Bockstael NE, Ivar ESJ, McConnell KE, Arsanjani F (1992) Sample selection bias in the estimation of recreation demand functions: an adaptation to sportfishing. Land Econ 66(1):40–49

Botzen WJW, van den Bergh JCJM, Aerts JCJH (2008) Report on a survey about perceptions of flood risk, willingness to pay for flood insurance, and willingness to undertake mitigation measures: explanation of the survey instrument

Boulware GW (2009) Public policy evaluation of the National Flood Insurance Program (NFIP). Ph.D Thesis, University of Florida

Bouma JJ, François D, Troch P (2005) Risk assessment and water management. Environ Model Softw 20(2):141–151

Brody SD, Zahran S, Maghelal P, Grover H, Highfield WE (2007) The rising costs of floods: examining the impact of planning and development decisions on property damage in Florida. J Am Plan Assoc 73(3):330–345

Brown MA (2010a) Anything but a breeze: moving forward without NFIP wind coverage. Boston Coll Environ Aff Law Rev 37(2):365–392

Brown OW (2010b) National Flood Insurance Program: continued actions needed to address financial and operational issues

J. Howard, II, *Socioeconomic Effects of the National Flood Insurance Program*, SpringerBriefs in Political Science, DOI 10.1007/978-3-319-29063-8

Brown PH, Tullos D, Tilt B, Magee D, Wolf AT (2008) Modeling the costs and benefits of dam construction from a multidisciplinary perspective. J Environ Manag 90:S303–S311

Bullock A, Acreman M (1999) The role of wetlands in the hydrological cycle. Hydrol Earth Syst Sci 7(3):358–389

Bullock JA, Haddow GD, Ergin DCE, Westerman L, Yeletaysi S (2006) Introduction to homeland security, 2nd edn. Butterworth-Heinemann homeland security series. Elsevier Butterworth-Heinemann, Burlington

Burby RJ (2001) Flood insurance and floodplain management: the US experience. Glob Environ Chang Part B Environ Hazards 3(3–4):111–122

Burby RJ, French SP (1981) Coping with floods: the land use management paradox. J Am Plan Assoc 47(3):289–300

Cheatham LR (1975) A case study of some economic aspects of the national flood insurance. Technical Report, Water Resources Research Institute, Mississippi State University, Starkville

Chetty R (2009) Sufficient statistics for welfare analysis. Annu. Rev. 1:451–487

Comfort LK, Cigler BA, Birkland TA, Nance E (2010) Retrospectives and prospectives on Hurricane Katrina: five years and counting. Public Adm Rev 70(5):669–678

Congressional Budget Office (2009) The National Flood Insurance Program: factors affecting actuarial soundness

Cooper C, Block R (2006) Disaster: Hurricane Katrina and the failure of homeland security. Henry Holt and Company, New York

Crowell M, Coulton K, Johnson C, Westcott J, Bellomo D, Edelman S, Hirsch E (2010) An estimate of the U.S. population living in 100-year coastal flood hazard areas. J Coast Res 26(2):201–211

Cutler DM, Zeckhauser RJ (1999) Reinsurance for catastrophes and cataclysms, Chap 6. University of Chicago Press, Chicago, pp 233–274

Cutter SL, Emrich CT (2006) Moral hazard, social catastrophe: the changing face of vulnerability along the hurricane coasts. Ann Am Acad Pol Soc Sci 102–112

Desvousges WH, Johnson FR, Banzhaf HS (1998) Environmental policy analysis with limited information. Edward Elgar, Cheltenham

Embrechts P, Klüppelberg C, Mikosch T (1997) Modelling extremal events. Applications of Mathematics, Springer

Farrow S (2011) Incorporating equity in regulatory and benefit-cost analysis using risk-based preferences. Risk Anal 31(6):902–907

Farrow S, Scott M (2013) Comparing multistate expected damages, option price and cumulative prospect measures for valuing flood protection. Water Resour Res 49:2638–2648

Frank RH (2006) Microeconomics and behavior, 6th edn. McGraw-Hill Irwin, Boston

Fraser JC, Doyle MW, Young H (2006) Creating effective flood mitigation policies. EOS Trans Am Geophys Union 87(27):265–270

Freeman AM III (1989) *Ex Ante* and *Ex Post* values for changes in risks. Risk Anal 9(3)

Godschalk DR, Brody S, Burby R (2003) Public participation in natural hazard mitigation policy formation: challenges for comprehensive planning. J Environ Plan Manag 46(5):733–754

Godschalk DR, Rose A, Mittler E, Porter K, West CT (2009) Estimating the value of foresight: aggregate analysis of natural hazard mitigation benefits and costs. J Environ Plan Manag 52(6):739–756

Griffith CT (1994a) The National Flood Insurance Program: unattained purposes, liability in contract, and takings. William Mary Law Rev 35:727–765

Griffith RS (1994b) The impact of mandatory purchase requirements for flood insurance on real estate markets. Ph.D Thesis, The University of Texas at Arlington

Haab TC, McConnell KE (2002) Valuing environmental and natural resources. New horizons in environmental economics. Edward Elgar, Northampton

Harberger AC (1978) On the use of distributional weights in social cost-benefit analysis. J Polit Econ 86(2 Part 2: Research in Taxation):S87–S120

Hellerstein D (1992) Estimating consumer surplus in the censored linear model. Land Econ 68(1):83–92

Herke J (1993) Teething pains at age 25: developing meaningful enforcement of the National Flood Insurance Program. Tulane Environ Law J 7:165–196

Hines JR (1999) Three sides of Harberger triangles. J Econ Perspect 13:167–188

Holway JM, Burby RJ (1990) The effects of floodplain development controls on residential land values. Land Econ 66(3):259–271

Horne J (2006) Breach of faith: Hurricane Katrina and the near death of a great American city. Random House, New York

Hubbard G (2012) Consequences of government deficits and debt. Int J Cent Bank 8(S1):203–235

Jones CP, Coulbourne WL, Marshall J, Rogers SM Jr (2006) Evaluation of the National Flood Insurance Program's building standards

King RO (2005) Federal flood insurance: the repetitive loss problem

Kleiber C, Zeileis A (2008) Applied econometrics with R. Use R! Springer, Berlin

Knabb RD, Rhome JR, Brown DP (2005) Tropical cyclone report: Hurricane Katrina. National Hurricane Center

Knabb RD, Brown DP, Rhome JR (2006) Tropical cyclone report: Hurricane Rita. National Hurricane Center

Kousky C (2008) Responding to risk: information and decision making in the floodplains of St. Louis County, Missouri. Ph.D Thesis, Harvard University, Cambridge

Kriesel W, Landry CE (2004) Participation in the National Flood Insurance Program: an empirical analysis for coastal properties. J Risk Insur. 71(3):405–420

Kunreuther H (2006) Has the time come for comprehensive natural disaster insurance? University of Pennsylvania Press, Philadelphia, pp 175–201

Kunreuther H, Michel-Kerjan E (2010) Market and government failure in insuring and mitigating natural catastrophes: how long-term contracts can help. The AEI Press, Washington, pp 115–142

Kunreuther H, Ginsberg R, Miller L, Sagi P, Slovic P, Borkan B, Katz N (1978) Disaster insurance protection: public policy lessons. Wiley-Interscience, Wiley, New York

Lambert PJ (2001) The distribution and redistribution of income, 3rd edn. Manchester University Press, Manchester

Landis ML (1998) Let me next time be tried by fire: disaster relief and the origins of the American welfare state. Northwest Univ Law Rev 92:967–1034

Landry CE, Jahan-Parvar MR (2011) Flood insurance coverage in the coastal zone. J Risk Insur 78(2):361–388

Landry CE, Li J (2011) Participation in the community rating system of NFIP: an empirical analysis of North Carolina counties. Nat Hazard Rev 13(3):205–220

Lawless RM (2005) Bankruptcy filing rates after a major hurricane. Nev Law J 6:7–20

Limpert E, Stahel WA, Abbt M (2001) Log-normal distributions across the sciences: keys and clues. Bioscience 51(5):341–352

Luebken U (2008) Die natur der gefahr. zur geschichte der überschwemmungsversicherung in deutschland und den USA. Behemoth A J Civilis 3:4–20

Marlett DC (1997) An evaluation of legislatively mandated residual market and catastrophe financing programs. Ph.D Thesis, Florida State University

Martin MA (2008) The impact of flood insurance on development in Ocean City, Maryland. Master's Thesis, Salisbury University, Salisbury

McLeman R, Smit B (2006) Vulnerability to climate change hazards and risks: crop and flood insurance. Can Geogr 50(2):217–226

McMillan CM (2008) Federal flood insurance polices: making matters worse. Houst Law Rev 44:471–505

Michel-Kerjan E, Kousky C (2010) Come rain or shine: evidence on flood insurance purchases in Florida. J Risk Insur 77(2):369–397

Michel-Kerjan E, de Forges SL, Kunreuther H (2012) Policy tenure under the U.S. National Flood Insurance Program (NFIP). Risk Anal 32(4):644–658

Moore DE, Cantrell RL (1976) Community response to external demands: an analysis of participation in the federal flood insurance program. Rural Sociol 41(4):484–508

Moss DA (1999) Courting disaster? The transformation of federal disaster policy since 1803, Chap 8. University of Chicago Press, Chicago, pp 307–355

Moss M, Schellhamer C, Berman DA (2009) The Stafford Act and priorities for reform. J Homel Secur Emerg Manag 6(1):1–21

Multihazard Mitigation Council (2005) Natural hazard mitigation saves: an independent study to asses the future savings from mitigation activities. National Institute of Building Sciences, Washington

National Research Council (2004) Analytical methods and approaches for water resources project planning. Technical Report, Washington

National Research Council (2010) A review of the proposed revisions to the federal principles and guidelines water resources planning document. Technical Report, Washington

Nicholson W (2004) Microeconomic theory, 9th edn. Thomson South-Western College Pub

Office of Management and Budget (1992) Guidelines and discount rates for benefit-cost analysis of federal programs. Technical Report A-94, Washington

Office of Management and Budget (2003) Regulatory analysis. Technical Report A-4, Washington

Orie M (2013) Case study 2. U.S. National Flood Insurance Program. The Geneva Association, Geneva, pp 23–28

Ramirez J, Adamowicz WL, Easter KW, Graham-Tomasi T (1988) *Ex Post* analysis of flood control: benefit-cost analysis and the value of information. Water Resour Res 24(8):1397–1405

Rose A, Porter K, Dash N, Bouabid J, Huyck C, Whitehead J, Shaw D, Eguchi R, Taylor C, McLane T, Tobin LT, Ganderton PT, Godschalk D, Kiremidjian AS, Tierney K, West CT (2007) Benefit-cost analysis of FEMA hazard mitigation grants. Nat Hazard Rev 8(4):97–111

Rumsey MA (2010) Beyond bigger and better: Gilbert White and America's new approach to floodplain management. Master's Thesis, Mississippi State University, Starkville

Sarmiento C, Miller TR (2006) Costs and consequences of flooding and the impact of the National Flood Insurance Program. Pacific Institute for Research and Evaluation, Calverton

Scales AF (2006) A nation of policyholders: governmental and market failure in flood insurance. Miss Coll Law Rev 26:3–47

Shilling JD, Sirmans CF, Benjamin JD (1989) Flood insurance, wealth redistribution, and urban property values incorporating distributional issues into benefit cost. J Urban Econ 26(1):43–53

Sirmans GS, Macpherson DA, Zietz EN (2005) The composition of hedonic pricing models. J Real Estate Lit 113(1):3–43

The Heinz Center (2000) Evaluation of erosion hazards. H. John Heinz III Center for Science, Economics, and the Environment, Washington

Titus JG (1998) Rising seas, coastal erosion, and the takings clause: how to save wetlands and beaches without hurting property owners. Md Law Rev 57:1279–1399

Tobin J (1958) Estimation of relationships for limited dependent variables. Econometrica 26(1):24–36

United States Geological Survey (2010) 100-year flood—it's all about chance. General Information Product 106

Viscusi WK (2000) Risk equity. J Leg Stud 29(S2):843–871

Water Resources Council (1983) Economic and environmental principles and guidelines for water and related land resources implementation studies. Technical Report, Washington

White GF (1942) Human adjustment to floods: a geographical approach to the flood problem in the United States. Ph.D Thesis, University of Chicago, Chicago

Whitehead JC (2006) A practitioner's primer on the contingent valuation method, Chap 3. Edward Elgar, Northampton, pp 66–91

Wooldridge JM (2010) Econometric analysis of cross section and panel data, 2nd edn. MIT, Cambridge

Yasui S (2005) A critical review of the tradition methodology of cost-benefit analysis and a proposed alternative. Hum Ecol Risk Assess 11:411–432

Yildirim U (1997) The decision to purchase flood insurance: a case study of Reno and Sparks. Master's Thesis, University of Nevada, Reno

Index

J. Howard, II, *Socioeconomic Effects of the National Flood Insurance Program*, SpringerBriefs in Political Science, DOI 10.1007/978-3-319-29063-8

MIX
Papier aus verantwortungsvollen Quellen
Paper from responsible sources
FSC® C105338

If you have any concerns about our products,
you can contact us on
ProductSafety@springernature.com

In case Publisher is established outside the EU,
the EU authorized representative is:
Springer Nature Customer Service Center GmbH
Europaplatz 3, 69115 Heidelberg, Germany

Printed by Libri Plureos GmbH
in Hamburg, Germany